Ten Million Steps on Route 6

A fresh look at America & Americans from Cape Cod to California

Joe Hurley • Travis Lindhorst

To Travis,
Hope you enjoy "walking" across the
country with me!

Joe Hurley
July 23-2018

ⓐ

ARKETT PUBLISHING
A division of Arkettype
New Milford, CT

10 Million Steps on Route 6

A fresh look at America & Americans from Cape Cod to California

written by Joe Hurley
photographs by Travis Lindhorst
(with additional photos from the public domain)

Second Edition 2014

Published by

ARKETT PUBLISHING
A division of Arkettype

PO Box 36, Gaylordsville, CT 06755
860-350-4007 • Fax 860-355-3970
www.arkett.com

ISBN 978-0-9816781-2-2

Printed in USA

On the cover: Joe in the Iowa Hills

Joe Hurley

JOE HURLEY is a retired newspaper reporter who spent most of his career at *The News-Times* in Danbury, Connecticut, where he wrote, among other things, the consumer-humor column called "Shallow Pockets".

He lives in New Milford, a small town in the Litchfield Hills in Western Connecticut, with his wife Pat. They have a grown daughter, Dawn, and son-in-law, Sam, who are the parents of their granddaughter Claire.

In 1999, Joe came to the startling realization that he knew almost nothing about the other side of the state, even though Connecticut is small enough to fit in the back pocket of Colorado or Nebraska. That year, photographer David Harple and Joe walked across Connecticut to give *News-Times* readers, and themselves, a better picture of their home state. That was the prelude to the coast-to-coast walk.

These days, Joe is pretty much a homebody, writing occasional stories for *American Road Magazine* and attempting to play basketball with other old guys who probably should have stopped long ago.

Travis Lindhorst

TRAVIS LINDHORST earned a BFA in Photography from Bowling Green State University in Ohio. He also has a two year technical degree in commercial photography. His passion is black & white, editorial and documentary photography.

At the time of the Route 6 walk, Travis was a 28 year old freelance photographer. The published images were captured on a digital Cannon Powershot G5. He also took along a Nikon F-100 and Rolliflex camera to shoot black & white images.

Raised in the mid-west, but currently residing in Brooklyn, NY, Travis has been working as a print producer in advertising for over 6 years. He still freelances now and then, but mainly shoots for personal enjoyment.

Acknowledgements

It would be impossible to thank all of the people who have contributed to the Route 6 walk and to the book. There are, of course, some people who would rather be in the background: Lou Okell, our book designer and Jim Slupatchuk our website designer. They could have made more money doing other projects but stuck with us. And Pat Hembrook, who helped get the project off the ground.

And our deepest thanks to:

• All of the people who walked with me. Some of you are in the book. All of you should be.

• My friends who visited me on the walk: Pat, Dawn, Pat, Evelyn, Sam, Ed and Eileen, Paula Goff-Moyer and Bill McIlrath. And those who called me, like Brian Durkin, or sent notes during the long nine months—and there are many of you.

• All the hotels, motels, inn, guesthouses and private homes who gave us room and some pretty darn nice breakfasts along the way.

• All of the people who donated money and other valuable things such as their life stories.

• The newspapers, travel bureaus and other organizations that paved the way for us as we entered their communities. Especially the folks at my own newspaper who backed the project early: Val Roth, Bill Sweeney and Paul Steinmetz.

• All the communities that greeted us so warmly, especially Meadville, Linesville, Sandusky, Nappanee, Gary, Hastings, Holyoke and Long Beach.

• And of course our volunteer proofreaders: Ed, Eileen, Tim, Dawn, Paula and Richard Saks. If you see any mistakes, don't blame them, call me. (Of course, I will pretend it's their fault.)

Dedications

This book is dedicated to the people who have shared our lives.

My wife Pat; my daughter Dawn; mom, dad, Mary, Pat, Evelyn and Tom. To my friends, Tim, Ed and Eileen. Without all of them I would not be who I am (for better or worse).

It is also dedicated to the people who supported this venture. Without them there would be no walk and no book.

And to an eighth grade teacher who will never know the impact she had on one young soul....

—Joe

This book is dedicated to my family—Bruce, Jocelyn & Clint. Your support cultivated a young man's need to develop his self-awareness and desire to explore the unfamiliar. I would also like to thank Magda for her patience and encouragement.

—Travis

Fond Memories

We have lost some of our favorite people since the walk. We miss them greatly.

Pat Hurley, my sister whom I seem to miss more and more each day. Time does not always ease the pain. My big brother **Tom**. And my nephew **Colin Goff**, who gave us our first map for the trip.

 **Dave Harple**, the chief photographer at *The News-Times* in Danbury Conn. walked with me through Connecticut—twice. Those trips were the inspiration for the cross-country walk. We spent all day together for days-on-end and I came to realize he was a better person than I. Anyone who knew Dave and his irrepressible spirit would miss him. I do.

—Joe

A special dedication is added here to my mother **Jocelyn** who passed away suddenly in November 2007. She was too young, too healthy and loved by too many. I now find solace in the fact that she is where she always wanted to be—among loved ones, watching over us, and still very much alive in our hearts. Miss you dearly.

—Travis

Route 6 Walk

March–December 2004

A Note From The Author

elcome fellow travelers. We are about to trek ten million steps (3,600 miles) across mountains, plains and deserts during summer's heat and winter's snow. Now here's the scary part: I'll be your guide, and I'm new at the job. So expect a few bumps along the way, but we'll share a great adventure as we explore our nation the old-fashioned way—by foot.

To make it easier, I've already done the walking part. I also wrote hundreds of essays during that walk from Cape Cod to California on Route 6, the longest highway ever created in the U.S. Many of them are in this book along with pictures taken by Travis Lindhorst, who was smart enough to drive instead of walk.

Along the way, we'll meet coal miners, farmers, banjo players, cowboys, country folk and city workers. They are the current generation of the extraordinary ordinary people who built this nation. They are the face America sees when it looks in the mirror.

And we'll see ducks that walk on fish, menacing cows, women in hard hats, a grand mirage, and the bravest little car in the world.

But mostly, we'll savor the places you don't find in the fast lane. You can visit Cape Cod a thousand times, but you won't understand the cape until you travel its back roads in winter. You can drive through Glenwood Canyon on I-70, but you won't experience it until you walk along the path next to the Colorado River deep inside the canyon walls.

Some of these stories were published in newspapers during the walk in 2004. They've been rewritten and updated, but I've tried to retain their original flavor. And there are many new stories, just to make sure you're getting your money's worth.

I hope you enjoy reading them as much as I enjoyed writing them. Actually, I hope you enjoy them more. Writing is hard work and requires much cursing.

More details of the walk—why I did it, what it was like, what lessons I learned and most importantly, how many pairs of shoes I wore out—can be found on page 240.

Table of Contents

MASSACHUSETTS

Bob Hazard

California's Just Ten Million Steps Away–Oh My!

I dipped my hand into the icy Atlantic Ocean and started walking west under drizzling gray March clouds. This was not a promising start, but I learned quickly that Cape Cod is paradise in winter.

OK, paradise should be a lot warmer, but if you head to the far end of the peninsula, you're alone with the waves, the sand and the wind. It's like finding a Monet under the graffiti of July crowds.

In winter, you can look out on Cape Cod Bay without a boat in sight. You can stop at a restaurant and actually find a seat. You can meet the year-round folks who avoid the towns in summer.

On the first day, I calculated that it would take 10 million steps to reach Long Beach, California 3,600 miles away—and my legs already hurt. As I walked past the cranberry bogs and marshes, I wondered what people would think if I quit on the first day. Fear of failure kept me going. Sore legs and the fear of failure would be my constant companions on the journey, one telling me to stop and the other urging me forward.

I followed Route 6A, the quiet side of the cape, which includes a long historic district that stretches all the way to the high arch of Sagamore Bridge. There are inviting bike paths on both sides of Cape Cod Canal, but after that, Route 6 heads west, through a long strip of motels, shopping centers and gas stations. You're just a minute from the ocean but you could be anywhere. There are too many Anyplace, USA, roads in our nation. Fortunately, most of Route 6 is more like the small roads on Cape Cod—except they're a lot straighter in the Midwest.

The Cape In Winter
Provincetown-Truro

Herring Cove is a beautiful stretch of fine sand (and nude beach) at the far end of the cape, right next to Province Lands National Recreation Area. This is where our journey begins.

At the edge of the Provincetown business area, there's a curious shop with a small yard awash in metal art: wrought-iron roosters, sailing ships, lighthouses and one big, angry snapdragon with menacing metal teeth. I wanted to know more, but alas, the artist wasn't there this chilly morning.

Then again, almost no one is in Provincetown in March—certainly not at 10 in the morning. Walk along narrow Commercial Street and you'll find more workers than residents. You'll see plumbers, carpenters and electricians getting businesses ready for the season. Nearly all of the shops are closed now, but in summer this little street will be a carnival crammed with tourists, summer residents, gay couples and gawkers.

You won't see Henry Bloch there in the summer. He's one of the few winter residents in nearby North Truro.

"In summer, this place is so crowded you don't go to town unless you have to," said Henry, who was coming to Truro for decades before he moved here year-round in 1990. For him, the lower cape (that's the far end of this curled-arm-shaped peninsula) is a slice of heaven in the off-season. He can walk over the dunes, look out onto Cape Cod Bay and see the world as it was long ago: ducks swimming in green water with a lonely boat or two off in the distance. No people. On special days, the waves freeze, transforming the ocean into giant ice sculptures.

"Some of them look like creatures with big teeth. It only happens a few times a year, but it's spectacular," Henry said.

At 77, Henry cherishes his solitude, but he misses the one person who shared his life on the cape. There's sadness in his voice when he talks

Albert Tinkham ready for Easter

about the years that his late wife, Jean, spent here as a girl. She loved the cape even more than he does. For decades, they walked the beaches together.

Now he walks alone.

Down the road about two miles, Albert Tinkham is a one-man celebration committee. Whether it's Halloween, Thanksgiving, Christmas, St. Patrick's Day or Easter, you'll find his yard filled with bright pinwheels, flags, balloons and other holiday displays. This week, he has Easter baskets, eggs and, of course, bunnies of all types and sizes.

At 73, you'd think Albert would let younger people do the work —and there's a lot of work to this. But he likes it. Especially at Halloween and Christmas, when kids prod their parents to drive by the display.

"You hear the cars stop and the kids are shouting. They're happy. I like that," Albert said. "I had 240 kids here for trick-or-treat on Halloween."

But it's not just for the kids. In Albert's living room you'll find more than 100 Easter bunnies he's collected over the years. They're everywhere: on the window sills, the counters, the stairs, the tables.

Albert is a legend on the lower cape. Two towns away, in Eastham, I met a family that always takes Route 6A on their way to Provincetown, just so the kids can see what's at Albert's place.

Albie, as they call him, is a Truro native who worked for years at the public-works department.

"This is the only place I've ever lived. I was born here and I'm going to die here," he said.

Until then, he'll keep putting smiles on thousands of faces.

At The Corners of the World
Eastham

n Orleans, the cape gets thinner, becoming a narrow strip of land. The heart of the national seashore is here, at Nauset Beach. For people who love the cape, this can be sacred ground.

Some visitors come to Coast Guard Beach and Nauset Beach for their huge waves. You can hear their thunder from Nauset light on a hill above the beach. But what really makes this spot special is a little shack that's not there any more. The lighthouse overlooks the marsh where Henry Beston lived when he wrote The Outermost House, the 1928 nature classic that paved the way for the creation of the national seashore. He's been called a founder of the environmental movement.

Working out of a primitive cottage, Henry wrote about his encounters with the waves, the creatures and the dunes. The ocean was at his front door and Nauset Marsh was at the back door. He stayed there during the worst weather to take nature's pulse. Beston's closest neighbor was the Coast Guard station.

Here's a passage from his book.

"In this solitary dune, my house faced the four corners of the world. Listen to the surf, really lend it your ears and you will hear a world of sounds...

Race Point Lighthouse

sometimes the vocal sounds that might be the half-heard talk of the people of the sea."

You'll find that passage on a plaque near the former Coast Guard Station. It's also a great spot to see the waves pounding below. If you go there in summer, bring money for parking—and hope the lot's not full.

You won't find crowds at First Encounter Beach on the other side of Route 6 in Eastham. This is where the Pilgrims met Iyanough, leader of the Cummaquid tribe while they were exploring the cape before they moved on to Plymouth. It was not a pleasant encounter. There's a statue of Iyanough in the city that bears his name, Hyannis.

If you want to see the first official landing, you can drive about 15 miles from the cape to Plymouth, where the famous Plymouth Rock still attracts and surprises people. They're surprised because the rock isn't as majestic as they expected. It's just a rock, folks, not Mount Rushmore.

The Quiet Side Orleans

Route 6 A twists along the bay side of Cape Cod. This is the quiet side of the cape: winding roads with antique shops around every bend, grassy fields, salt ponds, rivulets, tiny villages and bogs of rust-red cranberries. From Orleans to Sandwich, 6A is 34-mile long historic district along Cape Cod Bay.

"It's the longest historic district in the country," said Ken Traugot, owner of the Beechwood Inn in Barnstable village, the subdued neighbor of bustling Hyannis, the cape's biggest city.

On the quiet side, I spotted a trail to the Nobscussett Indians burial ground and stopped to pay respect to the people who nurtured this land centuries ago. The burial area was a small triangle of land overlooking a lake. Feathers, pinecones and shells formed a small memorial at the entrance.

A few minutes later I met Dick Buck peering at the lake with binoculars.

"Do you know the lake's name," I asked.

"Young man, I know everything there is to know about this town," said Dick, who admitted to being "somewhat over 60."

And with that, he offered to take me on a brief tour of his beloved hometown, Dennis. I'll go anywhere with someone who calls me young man.

We started with the lake: Lake Scargo, named for a mythical Nobscussett princess. According to legend, the tribe scooped out the land with clamshells to build a lake for Scargo's fish. They piled the soil next to the lake creating the highest hill on the cape.

"From the top of that hill you can see virtually all of the cape," Dick said. "And if you look down on the lake, you'll see that it's shaped like a fish."

Somewhere in the lake there's a Chevrolet Corvette, stolen by teens nearly a half-century ago. They drove the Chevy onto the frozen lake, had their fun, then sent it off onto the thin ice—where it sank. Dick said he's scoured the lake but never found the car. He knows it's there because he was living in Dennis when the whole affair happened.

Bass Hole Boardwalk at Grey's Beach, Yarmouthport

Dick drove me to the site of the former Shiverick Shipyard, where the company made clipper ships, the fastest vessels of their day. Along the way he told me the history of each house we passed. But one place made his blood boil. It was a mansion overlooking the ocean.

To Dick, the house is a symbol of the loss of human values on the cape: an ostentatious showplace where there was once a simple home.

"They spent a million dollars just to bring in sand so the new house would be higher," he said, estimating the house cost upwards of $7 million. "Not long ago anyone could walk through the surrounding land but the new owners don't want trespassers."

"You think we like that?"

Dick returned me to the lake where I continued my walk, but I learned he isn't the only native who resents newcomers and summer folk. In fact it's a theme.

"We're called wash-ashores," said Debra Traugot (Ken's wife) who moved to the cape a mere decade ago. "If you were born and raised here, I can see how you'd be resistant to change. But growth has brought in a lot of renewal. Summer residents and tourists help pay the taxes and keep the communities alive."

The Beechwood is a good example. The 150-year old Victorian inn was decaying until it was transformed into a bed & breakfast in the 1980s. The two beech trees that gave the inn its name are still there, but now the Beechwood is a haven where antiques share rooms with air conditioners and VCRs. If you really want a taste of the quiet side, just set yourself down on the wrap-around veranda and watch the world go by in slow motion.

Captain of the Islands
Hyannis

Ferry Captain Brian O'Malley

O n the ocean side of Cape Cod, the islands of Martha's Vineyard and Nantucket are sentinels guarding the peninsula—and magnets drawing tourists. Unfortunately most visitors don't make it much farther than the ferry ports of Vineyard Haven, Oak Bluffs and Nantucket.

You can spend a very nice day or weekend in any of those towns, visiting the gingerbread cottages in Oak Bluffs, the Black Dog Café in Vineyard Haven or Nantucket harbor.

But travel beyond the towns, and you'll get a different feel for the islands. You'll be able walk the beach between the ocean and the cliffs at Gay Head or try fresh—literally right off the boat—lobster at the fishing village of Menemsha or get bowled over by the waves at an ocean side beach. Nantucket is small enough that you can tour the entire island by bike.

Part of the fun is taking the ferry to the islands. After going through the hassles of traffic and parking on the mainland, you begin winding down on the boat—unless you're Brian O'Malley, the senior captain on the Steamship Authority's cargo ferry, The Gay Head.

"It's a great job, but you're constantly on your toes," he said. "Everything that happens on this boat is 110 percent my responsibility."

He's out there dealing with the weather every day on a boat that's 230 feet long and weighs 98 tons.

"When you have something like this that doesn't stop on a dime, you have to be very cautious," he said. "We go dead slow out of the harbor."

Even though he travels the same routes, the voyage is always different. The weather here changes almost without warning.

"The other day the wind was supposed to be 25–30 miles an hour. The front came in through Woods Hole at 50-to-55," Brian said.

In winter he worries about ice.

"There are times when the ferry just inches along in thick ice, even with a Coast Guard cutter clearing the way. It freezes over again very quickly," Brian said. "One year, we had ice four miles out (to sea). You'd get stuck, then back up and go forward, little by little"

In the summer, the harbor is filled with pleasure boaters who have no idea of how long it takes to maneuver a ferry.

When you ask Brian about the hardest part of his job, he'll tell you immediately that he never had enough time with his wife and daughters.

"My wife's been wonderful. When I was away half the time, she raised the girls by herself," he said.

Brian has been commuting to the mid-cape for decades. "Crossing the Bourne and Sagamore bridges in summer is a nightmare, but the winter traffic is no longer a picnic, either."

"That's been one of the biggest changes over the years. Obviously, the number of people has increased, and it's not just the tourists," he said.

Paul Noonan in his office

Parnassus Books
Yarmouthport

The Parnassus Book Service is on the quiet side of the cape, but it's really in a world of its own. Where else can you buy a paperback on the honor system, snuggle up with a children's book, and find a Russian novel—in Russian?

The big blue barn on Old Route 6 is like an eccentric professor's office. Books are everywhere. They're squeezed onto shelves that reach to the 15-foot-high ceiling. They're in piles on the floor, in boxes, on tables. You can't turn around without bumping into books.

And Paul Noonan knows where to find each one of them.

"We're known for our children's books, gardening, sculpting and painting books—but we should be known for a lot more," said Paul, who worked in the Harvard University library before landing the job at Parnassus, his lifelong dream.

The shop has thousands of nautical and marine books and thousands more on New England. It also has a large collection of Russian books, many in Russian.

"We get a lot of requests from Russia," Paul said as he picked his way through the shop, pointing out collections of military history, furniture, antiques, languages, arms and weapons, poetry and black studies.

"We had more black-studies books, but Maya Angelou came in and bought a lot of them. She bought a lot of our cookbooks too," Paul said.

You don't even have to go inside to get a book. There are thousands of paperbacks under a roof on the side of the building. Pick the ones you like and pay inside. If the store's closed, just leave a dollar in the mail slot.

Where else can you do that today?

What An Odd Bridge It Is

Sagamore to Bourne

A s I walked beside Cape Cod Canal my only companions were the gulls flying overhead, a few ducks in the green water—and one sneaky barge. The big blue-and-gray vessel slipped up behind me so quietly I didn't know it was there. I heard a soft churning

as quiet as a cat purring. I turned and the barge was so close I felt as though I could touch it. It was like suddenly being eye to eye with an elephant.

It will be very different here in the summer, when campers and picnickers jam Bourne Scenic Park, a camping and recreation area at the southern end of the canal. Park employees were already preparing for the onslaught.

"Winter is when we get most of our work done," said a park worker who was cleaning a catch basin.

When the seven-mile canal was built in 1914, it turned most of the cape into an island connected to the mainland by three bridges, but there's still a small slice of the upper cape on the mainland.

"There are some people who will say you're not on the cape until you cross the bridge. But there are people who live on Cape Cod who've never crossed the bridge—that's true," a local man told me.

Just down the road from the recreation area, Shaw's Fish and Lobster Restaurant sits in a prominent spot almost in the shadow of Bourne Bridge. But it's not the restaurant that catches your eye, it's the blue-and-white tugboat parked next to it.

Bourne vertical lift bridge.

Howard Shaw rescued the vessel from a tugboat graveyard, patched it up and towed it to Boston, where it was restored in 1982. Then it went to Buzzards Bay (through the canal, of course) where it was carried one mile over land to the restaurant. I'm guessing that the additional business from folks stopping to look at the boat has repaid Shaw's investment.

Most people think there are two bridges across the canal, Bourne and Sagamore, but there's a third bridge—and it's a real spectacle. I've never seen anything like it. Twin spires stand on each side of the canal, like giant Big Ben towers, connected by a span near the top of the towers. It looks something like an immense football goalpost, or the letter H—there's no way a vehicle can reach that span.

You wonder what the heck it is.

It's a railroad crossing. The tracks are lowered 135 feet when a train approaches. I've never seen the tracks coming down, but it must be quite a sight. This eye-catcher is the second-longest vertical-lift bridge in the U.S. For those keeping score, a bridge linking Staten Island to New Jersey is the longest.

Castle On The Hill
Fairhaven

 saw many diners on my journey (I like diners) but the Nest in Mattapoisett is special. It's a classic 1950s diner that still has its original fluorescent lights and terrazzo floors.

But it was the people that made the Nest memorable. I was a stranger walking into their midst, and they welcomed me.

Tom Brownell, who was having lunch with his daughter, invited me to join them. I had nowhere to stay that night so I asked where I could find an inexpensive place. He got me a free hotel.

Apparently that's the way things are in Mattpoisett.

"It's a great place for kids to grow up. There are a lot of activities for young people," said Cindy Stellato, Tom's daughter. On Thursdays hundreds of teens show up for a weekly dance on the wharf. And just this week, the town buried a time capsule.

Tom couldn't help telling me about neighboring Fairhaven, where Henry H. Rogers built the town a high school that looks like it belongs on the campus of Harvard or Yale. When the building opened, in 1906, it was called the Castle on the Hill.

Rogers, who was one of the wealthiest men in the nation in the late 1800s, was known as a ruthless businessman who built an empire in railroads, oil and gas. But quietly, often secretly, he funded projects such as schools in poor southern communities.

In Fairhaven, Rogers and his family donated a grammar school, an elaborate library, the town hall, a Masonic lodge, a church and an inn. They built the town's park, its water system and its sewer system.

I wonder what the people who were injured by Rogers ruthlessness would think about that. And I wonder what the people of Fairhaven think about the source of their good fortune. But that's another question for another time.

Fairhaven High School

The Witch of Wall Street
New Bedford

O n a good morning, you can walk along New Bedford's Fisherman's Wharf at sunrise and see sailors kissing their wives goodbye in front of their scallop boats. They're toting sea bags filled with heavy rubber boots, oilers (raincoats) and rain hats that look like flying saucers.

"There's a lot of activity here when there's a stretch of good weather ahead and boats are ready to leave," said Art Motta, the city's tourism director.

Fisherman's Wharf is part of a national historical park that stretches for 13 blocks in downtown New Bedford, once the world's whaling capital and the nation's richest city, per capita.

Just up the street at the New Bedford Whaling Museum, you'll get a sense of the enormous creatures that made the city famous. You can see the 66-foot-long skeleton of a blue whale hanging from the lobby ceiling; you can rummage around in a replica crew's quarters or let the child in you run wild in the world's biggest scale-model ship.

The whaling museum attracts more than 100,000 visitors a year. But few of them stop at the quirky, wonderful storefront museum just across the street. That's too bad. How could you not love a museum dedicated to Hetty Green, the most miserly woman in the world, according to Guinness World Records. She was also called the Witch of Wall Street and many other unflattering things.

Hetty, a New Bedford native, was the richest woman in the world and, a century ago, she was as famous as Martha Stewart is today. Five

Edith Nichols as Hetty Green aka the Witch of Wall Street.

songs were written about Hetty, including one by Irving Berlin.

The Hetty Green Museum could never compete with the whaling complex, but its founder, Edith Nichols, made my stop there more than worthwhile. She told Hetty's story with passion. She said that the press maligned Hetty because she was a woman who outdid the men at business. That was considered unladylike in the 1800s—maybe it still is.

"My goal is to tell people she got a bad rap," Edie said, explaining that the Witch of Wall Street nickname came from a reporter who was upset that Hetty wouldn't give him an interview.

Hetty was too busy for interviews. She started with a $7-million family whaling fortune and built it into a $100-million empire. She owned nearly all of downtown Chicago (she bought it cheap after the fire), a number of railroads (she gave her son a real train for his birthday), part of Fisherman's Wharf in San Francisco and a lot more.

"She was a very smart businesswoman. She studied everything before she invested. She bought low and never sold," Edie said.

Unfortunately, Edie's days of portraying Hetty were winding down when I visited. She had MS and was cutting back her schedule.

"If someone asks about the cane, I tell them I'm portraying Hetty after she had her stroke," Edie said.

She was trying to find another person with her passion, so Hetty's story doesn't fade away.

Edith Nichols died after my visit. Perhaps New Bedford will never know what it had and what it lost. The museum closed, but Art Motta, the tourism director, said the city is hoping to obtain and display the Hetty Green collection.

Like Hetty, Edie had a love-hate relationship with New Bedford.

"Edie felt she never got the support she needed," Art said. Although Art had disagreements with Edie, he never lost respect for her and the project she single-handedly kept afloat.

"She was very smart and likeable. She was an excellent actress and she knew everything there was to know about Hetty Green." In fact, it was sometimes hard to tell them apart, he said.

Farewell Edie.

New Bedford Harbor

Goodbye Lincoln Park

On Rt. 6 in North Dartmouth, I saw the ghost of Lincoln. Not Abe, just Lincoln Park.

Once, this was the most popular amusement area in southeastern Massachusetts, but today there are just a few ramshackle buildings under the eerie, decaying skeleton of the notorious Comet roller coaster.

The Comet, in fact, had a lot to do with the demise of Lincoln Park. Attendance dropped after a rider was killed in a Comet accident in 1986. The park closed for renovations but reopened with great fanfare the following year. But another coaster accident—a car jackknifed when the brakes failed—doomed the park.

Lincoln closed for good that December, nearly a century after the park was created to increase rail traffic in the area. It left behind tens of thousands of childhood memories and a laundry list of celebrity guests, including Eleanor Roosevelt and John Kennedy.

The bad luck continued even after the park closed: more than a half-dozen fires have left just a few buildings standing among the weeds. The jack-knifed coaster car stayed that way for years, until vandals tore it down.

Yes, there were problems, but folks who grew up around here treasure their memories of the Comet, the fun house and the old wooden carousel. They made Lincoln Park a rival of Paragon Park and Revere Beach, the major amusement centers near Boston. All three parks are gone now—but it was fun while it lasted.

The remains of the Comet at Lincoln Park

RHODE ISLAND

Farewell East Coast
Rhode Island

Rhode Island is a teeny state, the smallest in the nation, and it's dominated by a single city. Just about all of Rhode Island is a Providence suburb. No place is more than hour away from the capitol—or more than a half hour from the ocean.

In fact, Rhode Island—The Ocean State—has some of the best beaches in the Northeast. Unfortunately, Route 6 turns west at Providence and heads inland before reaching the beaches. No frolicking in the waves for me; I won't see the ocean again until California.

Rhode Island is also home to the ritzy mansions of Newport and to Block Island, which New Yorkers somehow think they own because it's so close to Long Island.

As Route 6 heads into Providence, it's more developed than in Massachusetts. But after Providence the shopping malls and motels give way to houses, forests and darn steep rolling hills. This is where Route 6 begins to feel like the country road that captures our fancy.

Providence

Providence is one of the nation's oldest cities and one of the first to embrace the industrial revolution. Its streets were built for pedestrians and horses. Many of its buildings are old factories.

In one of those factories, Xander Marro was working in The Dirt Palace, a women's art collective. This one-story brick building is a hub for music, handicrafts, film, architecture, puppetry and fashion design.

"We share a lot and help each other," said Xander, a 28-year-old drummer and puppeteer. "I'd just like to see everyone struggle less to survive."

Like many old cities, Providence's streets don't necessarily go where you think they should. I learned that the hard way. A bridge on Route 6 was closed, so I tried a shortcut. (My family shudders when I announce we're taking a shortcut.)

Sadly, after much walking, I wound up on a dead-end street. No problem. I cut through a scrap yard—and prayed there was no vicious junkyard dog waiting to attack. The shortcut cost me time and energy. The only good thing is that my wife will never find out about this misadventure.

Somehow, I managed to avoid all of the city's highlights, which include the nation's first Baptist church, Brown University and Providence College. Providence is also home to one of the most unusual sculptures in the nation—it's made of fire. WaterFire, an award-winning sculpture by Barnaby Evans, started as a New Year's celebration in 1994 and has grown steadily. There are now more than 100 fires on Providence's three rivers, and there are dozens of lightings throughout the year, usually on Saturdays at sunset.

On Westminster Avenue, beneath a rumbling elevated highway, I spotted Paul Seph, a Cambodian immigrant, selling fruits and vegetables out of cardboard boxes. Every morning, Paul buys his goods from a wholesaler and totes them to his stand.

"Everything here is the freshest, and the price is good," said Keita Sorib, a West African native, as she surveyed plantain, papaya, avocado and other fruits.

"Here you can get all the things you can get in my country. Here, I feel like I'm home."

A regular customer arrives and takes a piece of fruit without paying. He gets a nod from Paul and says thank you. Another regular drives up to show Paul her new baby.

Paul's just an old-fashioned American—from Cambodia.

Bird's Eye View
Johnston

West of Providence, I encountered a robin's idea of heaven: birdhouses of all shapes & sizes.

There's a 16-foot-tall mansion, a pagoda, a farmhouse, a castle with turrets and an apartment complex. They're just a few of the creations in front of Joe Danella's house on Route 6 in Johnston, where the city starts to fade into country. I saw my first deer on the trip near here.

Joe didn't have time chat with me; he was on his way out. Besides, I was only one of scores of people who come to his yard each week.

"People stop to look all day. It's continuous," said Joe, who makes the houses and sells them for $200 and up. His favorite is a 12-pointed star.

I was more interested in a bird church, complete with a cross. Our feathered friends seemed to be gathering around this one. Did they know today is Palm Sunday? Is there a service going on?

Wait, they're reading a sign in front of the church. It says, "The Beak Shall Inherit the Earth."

Danny's Auction Barn
Foster

ey, I've got a big roll of wire here," the auctioneer calls out in a rapid-fire cadence as he starts the bidding at $25.

"Who'll-give-me-25? 25? 25? Who'll-give-20? We have 20. Do we have 25? 30? Who'll-give-me-40? 40? 37-and-a-half? Got-37-and-a-half. Going once. Twice. SOLD!" he says tipping his cowboy hat.

Next up: metal cages.

It's just another day at the office for auctioneer Dick Laredo as he gets rid of tons of yard and farm equipment at Danny's Auction Barn in Foster, about 15 miles west of Providence and just a few miles from the Connecticut border. Later in the week, he'll be auctioning cars, parrots, horses, wrenches and hamsters. Maybe even a snake or two.

Danny Calise started the business 35 years ago, after working at other auctions. He's tried just about everything over the years, including country and western shows with big names like Freddy Fender, Brenda Lee and Earnest Tubbs. That didn't work out, but the auction business is booming.

Auctioneer Dick Laredo at Danny's Auction Barn

There's an auction just about every day. Today, it's farm equipment. Wednesday it will be cars: Thursday, farm animals and Friday, tools.

"On Saturday it's all general merchandise—anything you have in your house. That's a big one," Dick Laredo said. People come from as far as New Hampshire—two states away. Some of them just like to hear Dick's spiel.

"He makes people laugh. He was born to wheel and deal," said Stephanie Westgate, who has been working here since she was a kid.

Laredo isn't alone when he's trying to sell stuff. The merchandise owners aren't shy about promoting their goods. When a truckload of hay was stalled at $350, the owner tried to boost the price to over $400.

"Hey, where can you get 100 bales for 4¼?" he called out.

It didn't help. The final price was $350.

CONNECTICUT

A barn in Watertown / Inset—Joe and pals in Woodbury

Home State

series of hills greeted me as I entered Connecticut; they disappeared in the middle of the state but returned west of Hartford. As I climbed the hills

I realized that I should have walked from Canada to the Gulf Coast. The mountain ranges run north-south in the U.S., and I'll be crossing a lot of them.

Maybe I should have thought of that sooner.

Our journey through Connecticut begins in the Quiet Corner, the less developed section of the state where folks insist that economic booms always manage to elude them. Today, the area is mostly known for its two immense Indian casinos. There's also a lot of Revolutionary War history here and throughout the state. In fact, much of what is now Route 6 was a main road for Colonial soldiers, who avoided the coastal roads controlled by the British.

People in the Quiet Corner will tell you that the western side of the state, beyond the Connecticut River, is for rich people. Well, western Connecticut does have wealthy communities like Westport and Stamford. It also has the Litchfield Hills, where many New Yorkers have summer homes. But a lot of folks in western Connecticut are just trying get by. Trust me on that—I'm one of them.

American Clock and Watch Museum, Bristol

The Frogs That Roared
Willimantic

 People here apparently like a good joke. Why else would they put Volkswagen-sized statues of frogs on the main bridge into town?

It's not just the frogs; it's the tale behind them that tickles your funny bone. The story goes back a couple of centuries, and actually took place in a neighboring town, according to Willimantic historian David Haines.

One day, the villagers heard an enormous racket in the distance and thought natives were getting ready to attack. Quickly, they gathered a militia to protect themselves.

The ragtag platoon waited. The noise got louder. They waited some more. Finally, a scout went over the hill to see what was going on. When he reached the noisy spot, the scout saw that a dam had burst and thousands of frogs were high, dry, and croaking like crazy.

Somehow, this little story of menacing frogs survived for centuries. And now these amphibians are the town's mascots, guarding the bridge over the Willimantic River.

"I just think the frogs are funny," said Janet Haines, David's wife. "They've brought a lot of attention to the town." You can get frog T-shirts and all kinds of frog memorabilia downtown. In winter, they deck the frogs out in bright-red scarves.

The bridge is just a minute's walk from the old American Thread plant, the first factory with electric lights and, perhaps, the birthplace of the coffee break. There's some dispute about that, but Beverly York of the Windham Textile Museum, said the factory gave milk breaks to its child laborers. The adults, feeling left out, demanded equal time, and the coffee break was born.

The textile museum is across the street from the factory, housed in what was once the company store. Inside, you can tour a reproduction of a typical worker's house and examine furniture from the company manager's office. Another building holds a working spinning machine and other exhibits.

Next to the factory, the town has transformed the original Willimantic crossing into a flower covered walkway. And about a quarter-mile west there's a 640-foot long span across the river. The state claims that it's the only pedestrian bridge east of the Mississippi that crosses a highway, a rail line and a river.

Now, here's the strange part of this tale. As I was walking out of Willimantic, I heard ghastly sound on the other side of the road. I went over to investigate and, sure enough, it was frogs croaking.

And that's a true story.

Mark Twain in Hartford
Hartford

 Hartford is like the quiet child of two famous parents. It's about halfway between Boston and New York, and it feels more like a bedroom town than a hub. It's the capitol of the insurance industry.

That alone should tell you that the nightlife here is nothing like the bigger cities—or even New Haven, about 40 miles south.

But Hartford has its charms, from the rose garden in Elizabeth Park to the revived Connecticut River waterfront. And it's just a short ride to the ocean and mountains.

Just down the road, in Storrs, The University of Connecticut's men's and women's basketball teams are the state's pride and joy. Connecticut probably has more women's basketball fans per capita than any place on Earth.

Some people just plain fall in love with Hartford—like Mark Twain. Twain was born in Missouri (as Samuel Clemens), but he chose to live most of his life in Hartford. He wrote most of his books here, and he went broke here. That was after he built an eccentric house that reflected his eclectic life.

The house is now a museum where you can peek into the greenhouse where Twain played hide-and-seek with his daughter and you can see the porch where he hid from unwanted visitors while his assistant truthfully told them that Twain had stepped out.

Twain almost sounds like one of his fanciful characters. And his house is the same way—colorful and unique. No two elevations are the same. Gables that seem alike have different details. Chimneys and towers rise in unexpected places. There's even a lamp that Twain hooked up to a gas line with a tube that was the equivalent of today's extension cord.

The museum tells the story of Twain and his era. Manuscripts, photos and the architecture itself give us a sense of what made Twain perhaps the most American of our American authors.

Still, isn't it odd that a man famous for his Mississippi tales lived most of his life in a Northern city known for banking and insurance? He was born in Florida, Missouri, and spent his early years in Hannibal. But Twain's most popular works, including The Adventures of Huckleberry Finn, were written during his Hartford years.

The success of his books brought him wealth, but he didn't manage his money well. He had a habit of investing in inventions that never turned a profit. Facing bankruptcy (he used that porch a lot when bill collectors were at the door), Twain moved his family to Europe and later embarked on several international tours to repay his debts.

Even then, he called Hartford home. It wasn't until his daughter died during a visit to Hartford in 1896 that he soured on the house. He never returned after that.

Many of Twain's popular phrases are carved in the house's sandstone walls. Here are a few of my favorites:

- Nothing so needs reforming as other people's habits.
- We ought never to do wrong when people are looking.
- Man is the only animal that blushes. Or needs to.
- All good things arrive unto them that wait—and don't die in the meantime.
- Always respect your superiors, if you have any.

Hill-Stead gardens, (public domain photo)

Connecticut Time Machine
South Killingly to Danbury

I chose Route 6 for my cross-country walk because it's the longest (or second-longest, depending on how you calculate) highway in the nation, even though in many places it's simply a two-lane byway.

But in Connecticut I could have selected Route 6 for its history. The road is a time machine.

Colonial soldiers traveled what is now Route 6 during the Revolutionary War because inland roads were safer than the coastal highways, which were controlled by the British. Whether you're in Bolton, on the eastern side of the state, suburban Southbury, Newtown or Farmington, you'll see road-side signs marking the route that Count Rochambeau's army took to join George Washington at the Battle of Yorktown.

But that's just part of area's rich past. You could spend a week visiting museums on the 20-mile stretch from Hartford to Thomaston. In Bristol, there's a Carousel Museum, a clock museum (this area was the cradle of modern clock-making) and a small lock museum. The Mark Twain and Harriet Beecher Stowe houses sit side by side on Farmington Avenue in Hartford.

The Hill-Stead Museum is on a very steep hill in Farmington (the address is 35 Mountain Avenue). It's not directly on our route, but I hoped the Hill-Stead would give me a deeper understanding of Farmington's role in the Amistad trial. It was 4:30, but I gave it a shot and trudged up the hill.

When I arrived at the white-and-green mansion, there wasn't a car in sight, but a friendly security guard emerged and told me a little about the museum. After all that mountain climbing, it turns out that Hill-Stead has no connection to Amistad.

I could have learned more about Amistad by visiting Farmington's

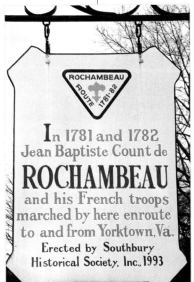

Historical Society or the Austin Williams House, which was built for the 53 Africans who were on trial for hijacking the Amistad, a slave ship that was taking them to Cuba. There are so many Amistad sites in Farmington that the town's Historical Society offers Amistad tours.

The Williams house, along with many Underground Railroad sanctuaries, is part of the state's Freedom Trail, which includes the Amistad Monument and a full-sized replica of the ship, both of which are in New Haven.

In case you were wondering, The Hill-Stead, an art museum, was designed by Theodate Pope Riddle—one of the first licensed female architects in the nation. That's enough to put the museum on the Connecticut Women's History Trail, a series of sites across the state that highlight women's achievements. Other stops include the Stowe house and the Windham Textile and History Museum, where visitors can catch a glimpse of the lives of women who worked in the mills.

The Prudence Crandall Museum in Canterbury is also on the trail. Prudence turned a sedate section of the state into an inferno when she opened a school for black girls in the 1830s. Townspeople shunned her, stoned the school and eventually set it on fire. The state passed a law banning the school, and Crandall was arrested when she wouldn't back down.

Prudence eventually won a series of court battles and had the ultimate victory—she's now the official state heroine. I felt connected to her in a small way when I spent a night in the Brooklyn, Connecticut, house where she stayed during the trial.

David Newell in Woodbury

Contrasts
Hartford to Danbury

Route 6 between Hartford and Danbury is a study in contrasts. You can walk past stretches of auto dealers, fast-food spots and convenience stores in places like Bristol, Thomaston and Danbury;

past farms and cow pastures in Watertown; or past rows of antique stores in Woodbury. The area has not yet merged into one big suburb. Hopefully it never will.

Just off Route 6 in Woodbury, you'll find the Glebe House, which claims to be the birthplace of the Episcopal Church in America. Today most people visit the small museum for its garden, which was designed by Gertrude Jekyll, one of the most important horticulturists of the 20th century.

Just down the road, an old-fashioned hardware store named C.L. Adams caters to farmers and celebrities alike. You can scoop nails out of bins for $1.40 a pound, purchase used furniture upstairs or buy enough hay to feed your livestock for months.

"We get two truckloads of feed—that's 46 tons—a week," said owner David Newell, who was a Woodbury schoolteacher before taking over the business his grandfather started in 1905.

But Newell says gentlemen farmers like Ron Howard and Michael J. Fox are customers too.

"It wouldn't be unusual for me to look up and see Arthur Miller buying a light fixture here. To us, he's just Art," Newell said of the playwright who has since died.

Up the road, you'll find the Charcoal Chef, where you just might walk into a Norman Rockwell scene of a bunch of guys sitting at the counter and trading barbs with the waitress. Not much has changed over the decades.

"The people here are the same as they've always been. They come in and get their own coffee in the morning. They pour their own juice," said owner Judy Doran, whose parents built the restaurant when she was kid.

It's the longtime customers that make Charcoal Chef an icon.

"We have one customer who comes in at 4:30 every day. He parks in the same spot; he sits at the same table and orders the same thing, a bacon-and-lettuce sandwich." Doran said, adding that he always reminds the waitress, "Bacon, well done." If he doesn't show up, they'll call his house to make sure he's all right.

Of course, there are fast-food places along the road and throughout New England. Dunkin' Donuts, with its pink-and-orange glass façade, is king. There are more Dunkin's than McDonalds, Burger Kings, Taco Bells, KFCs, Starbucks or even Subways. During a 20-mile stretch I counted five Dunkin's, four Subways, two McDonalds and no more than one of anything else.

There are no Dunkin's in Woodbury, of course. The town frowns on chain stores. And why would Woodbury want a Dunkin' Donuts when it has Phillips Diner? *Gourmet Magazine* called Phillips doughnuts the best in the county. Phillips is also regularly at the top of the doughnut list in Connecticut Magazine. Even the *New York Times* has written up this unpretentious little place where they only offer only a few varieties—plain, jelly, cinnamon and chocolate frosted—but they're all really, really good. Phillips changed hands recently and is now Dottie's Diner. But the donuts are the same. It's a tradition worth keeping.

Newtown Theater
Newtown

**Y**ears ago, when Tom Mahoney was a rookie movie-theater projectionist, the audience unexpectedly started laughing—rollicking, actually—during a Star Trek film.

"I was so nervous; I put the film in upside down. The audience was roaring, and I felt humiliated," said Tom, who survived that disaster to become head projectionist, night manager and finally manager of the movie house.

The theater is part—some people say the best part—of the town hall in Newtown, a quiet western-Connecticut town, where they still call the village green a pasture. It's one of the few theaters where you can watch a movie for two bucks and buy popcorn without reaching for a $5 bill.

Mahoney found his ideal job. He loves films and he loves the 500-seat theater where he saw his first movie more than 40 years ago. (It was a Saturday-morning kids' special.) He recalls watching his favorite film, *Raiders of the Lost Ark,* all alone in the theater on Christmas Eve. To him, that was a perfect night.

Today you might spot Tom sitting in the back row, watching the audience as much as the film. Or you might catch him greeting people and thanking them for coming as they leave the theater.

In nearby Thomaston, Paul Revaz knows how Mahoney feels. Paul is the technical director at a live theater on the top floor of the 130-year-old town hall.

"This area came very close to being converted into office space in the early 1990s," Paul said, as he surveyed the theater from a backstage perch.

Revaz took a small role in a play more than a decade ago, and has been with the theater ever since.

"It gets under your skin," he said, noting that the Opera House draws actors and audiences from most of western Connecticut. He's not sure what ures him to the theater, but it has something to do with the adrenalin-filled final week of nonstop rehearsals, and opening night.

Tom Mahoney in Newtown's town hall theater

The Edge of New England
Danbury

Danbury is the last New England community on Route 6. It's also where I worked for nearly 30 years The News-Times, and it was the home of the late Great Danbury Fair.

Our family spent many happy fall weekends at the big exhibition—the largest fair in the state and one of the largest in New England, with 100 acres of carnival rides, games, farm displays and parades—not to mention a 40-foot-high statue of Paul Bunyan towering over the fairgrounds.

The fair put Danbury on the map, attracting up to a half million visitors during its annual 10-day run. Busloads of New Yorkers trekked to what they considered the country, mingling with suburbanites and farmers.

Alas, the fairgrounds were sold in 1981. The fair was replaced by the Danbury Fair mall, which is, by far, the largest mall in the area. It has a Macy's, a Sears and other big stores. It also has a merry-go-round next to the food court as a gesture to the departed fair.

It does not have the Bunyan statue, which was allegedly moved to the site of the Woodstock Festival in New York and dressed as a hippie.

Danbury's other claim to fame, not counting the federal penitentiary, is hat making. Several hat makers had factories on the Still River, which runs right through downtown Danbury. The hatting industry declined when most men stopped wearing hats, but there was a time when everybody in Danbury knew someone who worked in the hat shops. The newspaper had a hat logo on its front page and the high-school sports teams are still called the Hatters—although I wonder how much today's teens know about hatting.

Just past the mall, Route 6 crosses into New York. With one step over the state line I've made it through New England!

The Danbury Fair was once the region's largest fall festival. Now it's a mall.

NEW YORK

WELCOME
TO
NEW YORK
The Empire State

A train crosses the Hudson River.

So Near, Yet So Far

e think of New York as skyscrapers and Times Square. But New York, the state, is rural. It's only about an hour from Broadway to farmlands. The change from city to country begins roughly where Route 6 winds and wiggles through a small corner of the Empire State.

That's a simplification, of course. There are pockets of development that have already swallowed up Route 6 and there are a few rural patches south of 6, but the road is a pretty handy dividing line.

Maybe that's because Route 6 is always about 50 miles from the city; or maybe it's because the commuter rail lines end at Brewster and Port Jervis, both on Route 6. It seems like everyplace on Route 6 is about an hour from the Manhattan—at 3 a.m.

Take Putnam County. It was rural not long ago, but now it's showing the strains of being a commuter's haven. There are new shopping centers and, of course, sprawl along Route 6 and Route 22 on both sides of Brewster. But there's still a lot of country nearby. The area is dappled with reservoirs which quench the big city's thirst. The protected lands around the reservoirs will always be green. As you get farther from the train lines and interstates there are still forests, fields and farms.

Cross the Hudson River on Bear Mountain Bridge and you've left the suburbs behind. Bear Mountain and a lot of other hills are ahead of you. The green Palisades Parkway is there too. And after you pass the New York Throughway at Central Valley you're in real farm country with tiny villages like Chester—but you're still just an hour from the city.

A solitary musician on the Hudson in Peekskill

Russian Orthodox
Mahopac

he Hermitage of Our Lady of Kursk in Mahopac is in a humble wood-frame house. The chapel is so small there's no room for seats, but it's a powerful reminder of the days when churches were grand.

You'll see more than 100 pictures, panels and icons in the two-room worship area, and you'll smell a mixture of candles and incense, even if you visit on a weekday, like I did.

Most of the people at weekend services are Russian émigrés or the children of émigrés. This Russian Orthodox parish was started in 1951 by· men and women who fled their country to escape religious persecution—just like the Pilgrims.

"The church was a central part of their daily lives," said Father Alexander Botschagow, the pastor here. Today, the weekend services are still in Russian, and most of the people in chapel are more recent émigrés. The grandchildren and great-grandchildren of the first émigrés have drifted away from the old church. Father Botschagow believes that's a part of modern society.

"It's a different age in America. We schedule everything around work. There's no leisure time; we try to do everything at top speed. We don't even have time to listen to each other," he said, recalling an era when families spent time together on weekends.

"When you push yourself like that, you push yourself away from God."

Maybe Father Botschagow has a different perspective because he straddles two cultures. His religious training is Eastern, but he was raised in New York City.

"I went to Catholic School, of all things, so I see both sides."

The hermitage is set back from the road about a mile east of Mahopac, a pretty little lakeside village. You're welcome to drop in.

The chapel in Our Lady of Kursk Hermitage

Painting Peekskill
Peekskill

 n Peekskill, on the eastern shore of the Hudson River, I spotted Samuel Bond restoring the entrance to a building on Main Street. Downtown Peekskill may have seen better days, but Bond is reviving one piece of the city.

Earlier this year, he refinished his brother Levi's storefront church, the Peekskill Christian Center. When the building's owner saw Samuel's work, he asked him to do the rest of the building. While I was there, a woman came by and asked Samuel to do her shop too.

"Samuel's secret?"

"You've got to get everything off with this wire brush," he said, scouring a section of the wooden door frame that looked perfectly clean. Then he slowly applied the varnish. It's hard work that takes its toll on the knees. But people appreciate the results.

"It's remarkable. It's like going from the Flintstones to the jet age," said John A. ("please put my initial in there") James, a member of Levi's congregation. "Look at it without the shellac," he said, nodding toward an unfinished area. "Nobody would want to come there. Now everybody wants to come. I call it a miracle. I call it the grace of God."

John moved to Peekskill to get away from the drugs in New York City. But he didn't find himself until he joined Levi's church.

"They were passing out flyers when they opened a here a year ago. He [Levi] touches you here," he said, putting his hand to his heart. "Then he touches you here," he said pointing to his head.

Levi and his wife, Sandra, are grateful to Peekskill, where people helped them when they were down.

"When we came here, we didn't have a place to live. We were homeless. A tear always comes to my eye when I talk about that," said Sandra, who is also a pastor. "We want people to know they can overcome anything."

She promised that visitors would be treated to a lively Sunday-morning service by a multicolored congregation.

The Christian Center is just a couple of blocks from the Hudson River, where there's a very nice riverside park. The city is trying to recreate itself as an arts center and has a number of galleries, shops and performance areas downtown.

Today, Peekskill's pride and joy is the annual Riverfront Festival, including tall-masted sailing ships in the harbor, dragon-boat races, concerts and lots of other activities down by the water.

Maybe Peekskill is coming back one step at a time, just like Samuel's buildings.

Samuel Bond paying attention to detail

A Majestic Crossing
Bear Mountain

When you cross majestic Bear Mountain Bridge, it's easy to imagine you're in the Rockies or the Rhineland, instead of just 40 miles upstream from New York City.

Just north of Peekskill, I walked up a steep mountain road that led to the bridge high above the Hudson River. As I crossed, I could see the river cutting through the green hills of the Hudson Highlands to the north. Below, the trains that rumbled along the riverside looked tiny.

To the west lies Bear Mountain Park. It's a small mountain, but you can see the Manhattan skyline from the summit and, on a clear day, you can pick out the Empire State Building.

Visitors love the mountain; they love the park's history, its famous visitors, its trails, its zoo, its museums and its bird sanctuary. Kids never forget the quirky carousel where they can ride on hand-carved Hudson River Valley animals.

All of that is nice, but here's what really makes the park special: a three-story fieldstone-and-chestnut grand lodge with big easy chairs where presidents, celebrities, hikers and city kids have watched the river roll by.

The lodge was built with local stone and logs in 1915. The park's founders wanted to create a gathering place similar to, but smaller than, the lodge in Yellowstone National Park. When it was done, the building was a masterpiece, with rustic birch timber, hand-hammered iron lamps, paintings of river steamboats, mounted animal heads and chestnut sofas.

Bear Mountain Lodge

The lodges at Yosemite and Smoky Mountains national parks were modeled after Bear Mountain.

Marilyn Monroe and Joe DiMaggio shared quiet dinners at the inn's restaurant. Bernie Williams, another Yankees star, sometimes stopped for a bite. Long ago, the Brooklyn Dodgers, the Giants, and the Knicks trained at Bear Mountain.

Franklin Roosevelt, Harry Truman, Richard Nixon, Ronald Reagan and Dwight Eisenhower visited the park. Probably not all at the same time.

Of course, you're more likely to meet everyday folks than celebrities here. It's a Mecca for Appalachian Trail hikers and, until the last few decades, steamboats ferried New York day-trippers up the Hudson to docks near the park entrance.

Only a handful of visitors come by rail (there are no stations close by), but from the lodge, you can see passenger and freight trains hugging the riverside. It makes a great picture.

"Train watchers come here all the time. They have their cameras and train schedules with them," said Bob Senerchi, who was walking down a quiet road through a riverside marsh near the tracks.

In early spring, the marsh is thick with golden reeds and birds. By midmorning, Bob recorded 37 bird species, including a relatively uncommon Virginia rail. He said that Peregrine falcons nest on Bear Mountain Bridge and swarms of eagles fill the sky during migration season.

"I love this place. It's an excellent spot for watching the bald eagle—I've seen 50 flying at once. It's something!"

Not far from the marsh you'll find the remnants of Doodletown, which got its name during the Revolutionary War, when British soldiers called the residents Doodles.

At about the same time, a man named Smith was stealing gold, silver and jewels from English supporters in what is now Monroe, west of Bear Mountain.

A lot of folks here believe the legend that Smith hid his treasure in the hills.

"I've been up and down these hills with a metal detector. I never found anything," Brian Barry said, with a shake of his head. Brian, his wife, Susan, and their daughter Meaghan ("nobody ever spells my name right") were out for a Sunday-morning bike ride on the Heritage Trail, which runs from Monroe to Goshen.

People here claim that Monroe is the place where Velveeta® Cheese was invented—or perhaps stumbled upon. Brian said workers made a mistake during the processing of a German cheese and wound up with the soft Velveeta. But there are several other versions of Velveeta's birth, including one by Kraft Foods, which claims it created the cheese. The Velveeta plant is long gone, but every year the town celebrates its most famous product with a cheese festival—cheese hats and all.

Making Money
West Point

Walk into a vault at the West Point Mint, and you'll see $100 million worth of gold bars stacked on the floor. That's the petty cash.

There's more than $20 billion stashed away here, in the nation's second-largest gold depository.

For ordinary people, the shiny bars are a spectacle. But for the employees, they're just heavy chunks of metal.

"The first day you work here, it's, 'Oh wow! Look at that,'" supervisor Joe Knox said. "But the luster wears off very quickly," added worker Bob Cooney.

That's probably because nobody gets to take any of the gold home. Everyone—workers, visitors, the mint police chief, and the plant manager—is scanned when entering the production area. The tiniest bits of metal, including the fillings in teeth and surgical pins, are recorded.

Everyone is scanned again when they leave—and they had better have the same amount of metal they had when they entered. There are no free samples at the mint.

If you haven't heard of the U.S. Mint at West Point, you're not alone. The building isn't set up for tours. Other mints have walkways where visitors can watch the process without disturbing the workers. West Point is too small for that.

That's too bad, because this little building next to the U.S. Military Academy is special. Even its birth is unique.

Inspecting coins at the West Point Mint

The mint got its start because the government misplaced three million Carson City silver dollars. The coins sat, forgotten, in a New York basement vault for decades until they were discovered in 1964.

The Carson coins—worth hundreds of dollars each—were sent to West Point, which shipped them to buyers. Until then, West Point had simply been a silver warehouse.

That was the first step to becoming a real mint. Within a decade, the plant was making pennies, centennial quarters and commemorative coins, like the gold $50 piece, which is worth about $400 today. If you're thinking of buying a few of them for $50 and reselling them, forget it. This mint sells coins at market value.

"We have a lot of pride in what we do here," said plant manager Ellen McCullom, whose favorite coin is the Library of Congress gold-and-platinum commemorative coin, minted in 2000.

"It's a very beautiful coin. It's really a work of art," she said, adding that it's difficult to join gold and platinum. "It was probably one of the hardest coins we've ever made."

Unfortunately, she didn't give me one as a keepsake.

For those keeping score, Fort Knox, in Kentucky, is the nation's largest gold depository.

Chariot Hall of Fame
Goshen

 **Y**ou could say the Harness Racing Hall of Fame in Goshen is an ode to a bygone time when horse racing was the king of sports. If you don't know anything about harness racing, think of Romans riding around arenas in chariots and you'll get the picture—except today's wispy chariots are built for speed, not combat.

But the Hall of Fame museum isn't mired in the past. When I arrived, dozens of kids were there for a birthday party—they loved this place. And why not? They got to walk through the paddocks and have their pictures taken in a sulky (chariot) with a whip in their hand.

The big attraction is the amphitheater where you're the driver in a 3-D race that seems so real that I ducked when mud from the horses' hooves sailed at me from the screen. Meanwhile, the seats twist, turn and vibrate with the sulky's movements.

"It's a bit like walking into Disney World," said museum library technician Patrick Newman. "People who haven't been here for a while say 'Wow, this place has really changed!'"

If you're wondering why the Hall of Fame is in a gingerbread building in tiny Goshen, just look next door at Historic Track, one of the nation's most storied trotting venues, and one of the few remaining active tracks.

Historic is the oldest trotting track in the world and has hosted many of the sport's biggest names, including Messenger and Hambiltonian. It was the first New York track where betting was permitted and the first

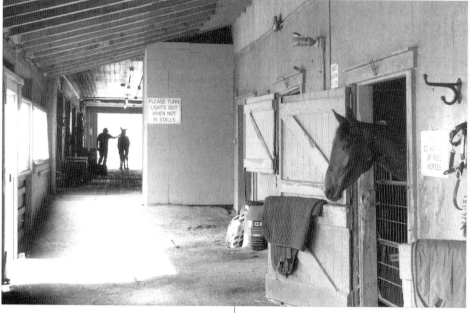

half-mile track on the Grand Circuit, harness racing's main tour.

But all of that history takes a backseat to the track itself, with its genteel covered grandstand, its stately oak trees, the fields where harness-racing greats grazed and the working blacksmith shop. Look around and you'll find plaques and statues commemorating some of the champions. If you come at the right time, you'll see today's drivers and horses training at the track.

Back in the museum, Ernest Zocchi, 69, was having as much fun as his grandchild.

"It's wonderful. You can see the history of racing from the very beginning to modern times," said Ernest, who grew up in Tuckahoe, New York, just a stone's throw from Yonkers Raceway.

"I used to go there when I was a kid. I've seen a lot of racing in my time," he said, recalling the days when he and his friends would sneak down to the track-side to hear the roar of the crowd mixed with the thunder of the horses as they approached the finish line.

"I went back there a while ago and it wasn't the same. There weren't many people in the stands," he said.

They're all at the casinos now.

PENNSYLVANIA

The Midwest Starts Here

 **W**elcome to Pennsylvania, where the East meets the Midwest. West of Scranton, Route 6 is dotted with small towns tucked in the hills far from the interstates. It doesn't look much like the Midwest, but it feels like it. This is where a guy who was whittling an axe handle called for me to come over and set a bit. And it's where another old-timer checked our Geo Metro and discovered it was out of oil. When you reach the Allegheny Plateau, the hustle of the Northeast is far behind you.

Unfortunately, Pennsylvania was also the state where I was attacked by my own belt. I stepped on the buckle after taking a bath. The prong was straight up, like a rattler poised to strike—and it bit me good. I could feel it hit bone, and there was a lot of blood. I don't like blood. Foolishly, I was on the road again the next morning. It rained like crazy, of course. I bought bandages at a drugstore near Honesdale, one of those small Pennsylvania towns. Soaking wet, I sat down in the store, took off my shoe and my bloody sock, dried my foot with tissues, and put the bandages on. I'm sure the owner was just thrilled to have me there.

We all know Pennsylvania is a coal state, but it's also oil country—at least it was until bigger deposits were found in Texas. The first oil well in the country was drilled in Titusville, and there are still plenty of little wells in backyards, parking lots and even cemeteries in the Allegheny area.

West of Meadville, the land flattens out a bit and begins to actually look like the Midwest—but with a lot more trees.

The Meadville Tribune

Small Towns
Hawley to Smethport

As you enter Pennsylvania, Route 6 runs through small communities like Hawley and Honesdale, then dips south toward Scranton before heading west to more villages.

Step into these little towns and you can feel the slower pace. People have time for each other. Folks greeted me as I walked along; they beeped as they drove by; they stepped up to offer encouragement, water, sport drinks and food. I was part of the family.

In Tunkhannock, in the Endless Mountains of northern Pennsylvania, Raymond Sands saved us from disaster when he insisted on checking the oil in our car. It was nearly dry.

Maybe somewhere else it would seem odd to have a stranger say "Let me check your oil." But here, it was just a neighborly thing to do, and Raymond likes to tinker. His red 12-year-old pickup truck was a mobile warehouse, filled with curiosities and gizmos that he picked up at auctions.

"I use these ratchet straps to hold down a load on my truck," he said, pointing to a box full of thick cloth straps. "This here pole is used to hold a four-by-four in the ground—that metal box would make a nice little flower pot," he said, pointing to a shiny rectangular bin on the passenger's side of the truck.

"Here's my spare tire," he said, picking up a mechanical inflator next to the would-be flower pot. The big old milk can is for a relative who collects things like that.

He doesn't worry about someone walking off with his unguarded goodies.

"There's not much there worth stealing." When I started this adventure, I wondered whether Americans had changed over the decades. I'm beginning to think that maybe we haven't changed, maybe our world has changed. It's a lot faster and more impersonal.

But in the hills, change comes slowly. The communities are too small to attract the kind of development that has transformed much of the East Coast, probably because they're far from the interstate highways. Potter County had 19,000 residents a century ago. Now it has 17,000. The whole county has fewer people than the little Connecticut town where I live. Forget your cell phones, they rarely work here. Forget your laptop; it's hard to find internet access. To an outsider, towns like Tunkhannock, with its wooden buildings and its old movie theater, look a like a 1950's photograph. And folks like it that way.

"I spent 16 years scrimping and saving to get out of here," said Teri Batterson, who lives in the village of Galeton. "Then I spent the next 16 years scrimping and saving to get back."

Teri lived in Denver, in Athens, Greece, and in Virginia Beach, but she missed the hometown feel of Galeton, where everyone knows your name.

"In Virginia, I was shopping in the same supermarket for four years and I realized no one ever called me by name. No one ever said, "Hey Teri, what's shakin'?" she said.

It's that way all through these northern counties.

"It's quiet here," said John Arzberger, as he stood outside his home in Mainesburg, which is just big enough for a general store. Just a few yards away, his daughter and a friend were playing in a stream that runs under Route 6. Twenty years ago, John swam in the same spot.

"It's a lot better now that the town built a sewer plant. It really cleaned up the water," John said.

John works in construction for one of the town's two big employers. Business isn't as good as it was a few years ago, but he plans to stay in Mainesburg.

In Troy, an innkeeper told me it's difficult to keep the young people here because there's not much work for them. Even the farms are having a tough time.

More tourists would mean more business, but he has mixed feelings about that: too many tourists could change the town he loves. He likes the small-town atmosphere where a little-league game is a big deal and three or four cars at a light is a traffic jam.

And that brings us back to where America is today. Something's gained from our modern world with its many choices, but something's lost, too.

As I walked through Massachusetts, Rhode Island, Connecticut and New York, only one person offered me a ride. After two days in the Pennsylvania hills, I had four offers. It must be nice to live in a place where people feel safe enough to do that.

The Stourbridge Lion
Honesdale

**W**alking along Honesdale's old main street, you wouldn't guess this little town is the birthplace of the American railroad—until you stand in front of the Canal and Railroad Museum and see a gawky locomotive staring at you through a picture window.

This big black beastie with red-trimmed wheels and a yellow lion's head painted on front is a replica of the Stourbridge Lion, the first locomotive operated in America. It has a sad little story to tell.

After the War of 1812, New York needed cheap coal for its growing industries. There was plenty of anthracite in the Moosic Range near Honesdale, but getting it to the city was an ordeal. In 1825, entrepreneurs built the Delaware and Hudson Canal to ferry coal from the hills to Hudson River, where it could be barged to New York.

"It was the little sister of the Erie Canal," said Sally Talega, director of the Canal and Railroad Museum right at the western end of the canal.

Of course, the coal had to get from the mountains to the canal. First mules, and later, tow ropes powered by engines, hauled coal cars up the western side of the Moosics. From the top, the cars rolled to the canal by gravity.

It was a cumbersome process, so in 1829 the Lion was imported from Stourbridge, England, to carry the coal up the Moosics.

Alas, the Lion was too fat. It weighed seven tons, and the tracks were designed to hold four. Its first trip was its last—it was just too heavy. The owners retuned to the gravity system and operated the

Coal chips in the Moosic Range

canal successfully until 1898, when they transformed the business into a railway company. The poor Lion was eventually dismantled and sold for scrap.

But there's a happy ending to our story. The Lion's one run was the first commercial train trip in the U.S. Because of that, the engine's boiler was rescued and is on display at the Smithsonian Institution in Washington. And, of course, the replica is alive and well at the museum.

The Lion lives on!

Honesdale is a quiet town today, but it has a cosmopolitan flavor, thanks to the international Himalayan Institute on a 400-acre campus not far from Main Street. The institute was founded here in 1971, as a retreat and teaching center by Swami Rama from the Himalayas. The group now has sites in a number of cities in the U.S. and several other countries. Don't be surprised if you see some of the students in town dressed in saris.

By the way, when you're traveling through this area on Route 6 you're pretty much following the old railroad route from Honesdale to Carbondale. While you're making that drive, look for the 200-foot-high windmills churning on the distant hilltops. They're supplying the energy we once got from coal.

Dying For Coal
Scranton

 f you were in the Lackawanna Coal Mine a century ago, you'd meet a little kid with a coal-dust black face. He'd be one of many six-, seven-, and eight-year-olds working in the darkness for pennies a day.

For most of them, it was the start of a career that offered low pay, debt, hard labor and black-lung disease. The Industrial Revolution—the world we know today—was fueled by their work.

This story is a thank-you note to the miners who helped build our prosperity. I could send the note to almost any family that has roots Scranton.

"My dad worked in the mines, my grandfather worked in the mines," said Lee Ruch, a former foreman at Lackawanna. Lee followed his elders into the tunnels. Now he, too, has black-lung disease. "You can't work in the mines for any length of time without getting it," said Lee, who labored in the mine fields south of Scranton for more than two decades.

"I loved it. I loved the challenge, the danger. You're standing on a one-inch-thick board, holding a drill over your head, putting holes in the coal."

Today, folks travel into the Lackawanna tunnels for fun. The mine closed in 1967, but Lackawanna County transformed it into a tourist attraction.

As you ride a mine cart down the steep shaft, you'll see the entrance gradually get smaller, then disappear. At the bottom, you'll chill in the 50-degree coolness and walk through tunnels

Trolley to the coal mine

carved out by workers decades ago.

Above, wooden beams hold the anthracite in place. Below, you walk on corridors where mules once hauled carloads of coal. Many of the mules spent their entire lives underground and were blind.

The humans' lives weren't much better. Before the unions, miners were independent contractors with no benefits and few rights. They worked alone or with a helper and were paid according to the amount of coal they produced. They purchased their own equipment, and they paid their helpers' salaries. Their wages were in company script, so they bought everything in the company store, where prices were high. Most of them lived in company houses.

A worker in a good section of the mine could fill several carloads a day. Less fortunate workers would crawl uphill into two-or three-foot-wide seams to scrape out small amounts of coal. Other than the faint light from their miners' caps, they worked in pitch-black darkness. If you're in the mine when the lights are out, put your hand in front of your face. You won't see it.

The workers fed the mine's rats, because the rodents could sense a tremble before humans. "When the miners saw a bunch of rats running, they'd run too," tour guide Merlin Phillips said.

Most of the miners were European immigrants and their descendants, who came to the Scranton area when coal fueled the nation's homes and industries.

"In the early 1800s, this was one of the first industries in the valley, it was all the immigrants had," Phillips said.

Today, the Lackawanna mine property has been converted into McDade Park, a local recreation area, including a Mining Museum and the mine tour, which attracts about 65,000 visitors a year.

Steamtown
Scranton

Ralph Coury was born in Scranton, a city built on coal, iron and railroads. Ralph's grandfather was a miner who had black-lung disease. His father was a trainman whose lungs were contaminated with asbestos.

You might think Ralph would want to get away from Scranton, but he loves the city. He loves the coal and iron in the city's blood. Most of all, he loves the railroad.

"I have a real passion for this place," said Coury, Public Affairs Officer at Steamtown National Historic Site, a renovated railroad yard operated by the National Park Service.

Coury's not alone; many of the people who work at Steamtown love the place.

More than 100 volunteers help Park Service employees run the 62-acre site that was once the home of the Delaware, Lackawanna and Western Railroads.

They share a passion for the days when Scranton was a rail center for the east coast. Just north of Scranton, Carbondale got rich by shipping coal by canal to New York. To the south, Wilkes-Barre had the Susquehanna River.

Scranton had coal and iron, but no water transportation. The rails gave Scranton the outlet it needed. Soon the city was a railroad hub—all westbound trains from New York went through the Scranton yards.

Today, more than 100,000 people visit Steamtown each year. Most will tour the roundhouse where trains went for quick service. They'll watch mechanics rebuilding engines and

An engine enters the roundhouse

perhaps take an excursion on an old train.

"I think people want to return to a simpler time, when things were less complicated," Coury said, explaining the 10-year-old site's popularity.

The most beloved exhibit, Big Boy, is actually outside the museum, near the parking lot. Big Boy is a 133-foot-long glistening black giant engine. Like all of the old-timers, he's full of gears levers, rods and chambers that make it a child's wonderland and a mechanic's nightmare.

Once a year, Steamtown allows people to climb aboard and sit in Big Boy's 25-foot-high cab.

"I'm amazed at how long the lines are for that. People just want to feel what it's like up there," Coury said. But his favorite exhibit is a working model of the rail yard on the second floor of the museum.

"That's the way these yards looked in the 1930s," he said, as the tiny trains went back and forth, recreating the activity of the yard at its peak.

There are times when Ralph wishes he was alive back then—when the railroad was king and Scranton was a hub. But that's not surprising coming from someone with Scranton in his blood.

Endless Mountains
Tunkhannock to Mansfield

 As you enter Tunkhannock, there's a sign that says, "Welcome to the Endless Mountains." It's not exactly what you want to see when you're on foot.

The Endless Mountains are low, but the views are wonderful. On overcast days, the clouds cover the hilltops and seem to tumble down the hillsides, like whipped cream on a dark-green sundae. On a gray, drizzly Wednesday morning, clouds settled in the dales and valleys west of Ansonia, covering them with a fluffy cotton blanket. Unfortunately, I was outside the blanket, shivering in the rain.

This is farm country. Above Wyalusing, a hill rises above green fields. At the foot of the hill, the gray Susquehanna River makes a long, lazy turn south. In the distance, haze covered hills stretch 10 or 20 miles into the horizon—the Endless Mountains.

Farther west, fields of dark and light green stretch beneath Sylvania Mountain, unmolested by power lines. In the moments when there are no cars, you can hear your footsteps or perhaps the hum of a distant tractor.

Now I'm sitting on a hillside guardrail taking in the atmosphere with a cool breeze washing over me. In the valley below, there are 20 horses in a field next to a barn with two white silos. Two of them are necking like lovesick teens. Others stand at attention, like bulls ready to charge, as a stranger walks by. One horse rolls in the grass and another scratches his back on a post. But most of the horses are content to search for morsels in the young spring grass.

It's a nice life.

Farm fields near the Susquehanna River **53**

Ghost Story
Wellsboro

**G**eorge, the ghost who likes women, lives behind a heavy black iron door in the old county jail in Wellsboro.

Yes, this is a ghost story, but the ladies who work on the other side of that big black door swear George is real. They've heard him walking around at night. They've heard him making strange noises. Once, he even asked a visitor what she was doing there.

The strange thing is that George haunts only women. He never does his spooky deeds when men are around.

"We think that's because the three men who were hung here, were hung for crimes against women," said Ruth Ann Shumway, who works the other side of the door, which is now the Tioga County Visitors Bureau. Even if you don't get to meet George, the ladies will be happy to greet you and tell you about this small town with a wide main street, a popular diner and lots of little shops.

The bureau's other women, Sandi Spencer and Lori Copp, said the unsettling noises are as close as they ever want to get to George. But Ruth Ann finds him fascinating.

"The others are afraid, but I'd love to meet him and have a conversation," Ruth Ann said, adding that no one knows exactly who George is, but they had to give the ghost a name and George seemed as good as any.

Perhaps George is just a fanciful tale created to explain strange noises in a former jail. But I've been in the back room by myself, looking at the four cells, at the metal ceiling and at the iron stairway and listening to the strange chirping of a cricket. I wouldn't want to spend a night there alone.

The only thing worse would be finding out that I wasn't alone.

A Triple Play
Sweden

ere's something you won't see very often. Denton Hill is just 2,500 feet high, but it's the only triple continental divide east of the Mississippi. In fact, there are only a handful of places in the world where water flows from a summit into three different major lakes or ocean basins.

Water from the Denton Hill feeds the Allegheny River, which flows west to the Mississippi and eventually to the Gulf of Mexico. Denton Hill is also the start of the Genesee River, which flows north into Lake Ontario. And it's the start of Pine Creek, which becomes the Susquehanna, which flows southeast into Chesapeake Bay. You can read all about it on a sign at the top of the hill.

Denton Hill
Sweden Valley

est of Galeton, Route 6 climbs the notoriously long Denton Hill where I met Christl Hoffert, who was also walking along the road. "I like the exercise," she said, making me feel pretty wimpy for trudging up the hill as though it were Mount Everest. But it turned out that she was only walking a short distance. (Hah! I'm tougher than her.)

Christl and her husband have a cabin on the hill. They're here for some family time with their son, who's scheduled for a tour in Iraq next month.

"Here, it's so easy to forget everything," said Christl, who hopes to move here permanently some day.

One of the things Christl would like to forget—actually erase—is her son's experience with the Marines.

"We're not happy about that," she said, adding that the Marines told her son that he wouldn't be shipped to Iraq when he joined a year ago. They told him he could change his mind, but when he did change his mind, they said he couldn't, she said.

"He went to cooking school, now they've got him in the infantry. If we could hide him away and put him someplace else..." she said, leaving the thought unfinished.

Wouldn't it be nice if the old folks who make the wars, were the first to go out and get shot at. I bet we'd have fewer wars.

The Middle Ridge Methodist Church near Wellsboro, built in the late 1800's, is made of wood painted to imitate brick.

55

Grand Canyon?
Ansonia

f you're traveling through the Endless Mountains, spend some time at Pine Creek Gorge.

The travel brochures call it the Grand Canyon of Pennsylvania, but don't expect a smaller version of that other canyon out west. Pine Creek deserves its own spotlight, not the reflected glory of a far-away spectacle.

The beauty of Pine Creek is that it's so accessible. You can drive to the East Rim, then check out the West Rim and be back in nearby Wellsboro for lunch.

You can stand eye to eye with the hawks as they soar 800 feet above the canyon floor. You can hear the muffled roar of Pine Creek far below.

"Just look at the mountains, the trees, the water, the birds flying. I didn't think it was going to be this beautiful." said Ken Siford, who drove from Cleveland with his wife, Lanette. She's lived in Pennsylvania for years, but never knew the gorge existed.

And they only saw it from the top. Many visitors take a covered-wagon ride along a trail that hugs the creek at the base of the canyon. If you're more adventurous, you can cover the trail on horseback or bicycle. This is where you'll see the deer, the otters, the wild ducks and maybe a bear or two. The air will be crisp and clean, and you can touch the river. Better yet, you can run the rapids on a canoe or kayak in spring when the water's high.

They could call this place Peaceful Canyon—but not in October, when the leaves are changing. That's when up to 8,000 people a day visit the gorge.

Pine Creek Gorge

Rain, Rain
East Smethport

It was a wet week in northern Pennsylvania. The area went through nearly a decade of drought, but the past two years have turned the other way.

That's what Oakley Colley told me as he surveyed his property after a flash thunderstorm dumped inches of rain in just a few hours.

In East Smethport, Robert Dunn was shoveling a thick layer of mud and rock off his sidewalk as though it were snow. The rain had washed roadside gravel down Route 6 to the bottom of the hill, where Bob lives.

"It was a hell of storm," Bob said. "They even had the snowplows out last night, plowing the dirt and water off the road."

Bob hadn't seen it this bad since he bought the house just after Potato Creek flooded in 1972.

About a half mile down the road, Route 6 passes over Potato Creek, just after it merges with Marvin Creek. The river was running so fast that I got dizzy looking straight down into the muddy brown water.

Alongside the creek, Walter Arthur and Joshua James were working on a pickup truck. Walter's had a rough time lately, but he had enough compassion to think about someone else when he saw me without a raincoat on a day when another storm was in the air.

"Here, I don't have much, but take this," he said, handing me a dollar bill and small emergency poncho in a pouch.

Things like that aren't unusual around here. I get offers of rides nearly every day. Today, a woman gave me $10 to buy a decent dinner.

People here aren't affluent. There's not much steady work. When you pass through these towns you think you've returned to the 1950s—and, in some of them, you see a lot of vacant storefronts. But the people here are proof there's more to life than money.

The wet and lonely road

Quaker State Oil
Warren, Pennsylvania

I t's a little strange to think of Pennsylvania as oil country, but Pennzoil, Quaker State and Kendall all got their start here. Edwin Drake drilled the nation's first oil well nearly 150 years ago in Titusville, on the western side of what is now the Allegheny National Forest. And Drake's well produced only a trickle compared with the oil that was later pumped from land near Bradford, on the eastern side of the forest.

Jim Bryner

Commercial drillers flocked to Bradford, making it the nation's oil capital. There were 90,000 active wells in and around Bradford at the turn of the century—on farms, in backyards and even in graveyards.

In one year, 85 percent of the nation's oil production came from the Bradford fields. Even though larger fields were discovered elsewhere, Bradford remained an oil hub because its oil was rich in paraffin, an ideal lubricant.

The oil was trapped in small veins in sand more than 1,000 feet deep. Drilling rigs dotted the area. Inside the rigs, heavy drills were raised 72 feet and dropped, to create and deepen the wells. Later, explosives were packed into the hole to help free the oil.

For oil workers like Jim Bryner, this was a good job.

"It would be considered dangerous today, but we didn't think of it that way," said Jim, who worked in the Bradford fields during the Great Depression.

The standard pay was $122.50 a month, a nice wage back then.

"We thought it was a great job; we were out in the open air. We had a lot of pride in what we did." But even Jim didn't care for the winters. "I can remember when it was 40 degrees below—and you didn't stop because of the weather," he said.

These days, Jim is a guide at the Penn-Brad Oil Museum, a little exhibit just outside Bradford, where you can take a short tour inside an old drilling rig. That's nice, but having a guide who actually did the work makes it a lot better.

There are still a number of active oil wells in the Bradford area, and people around here say the high price of oil is luring the independents back to the fields.

The drilling rig at Penn-Brad Oil Museum

Ed Fox, Whittler
Hazel Hurst, Pennsylvania

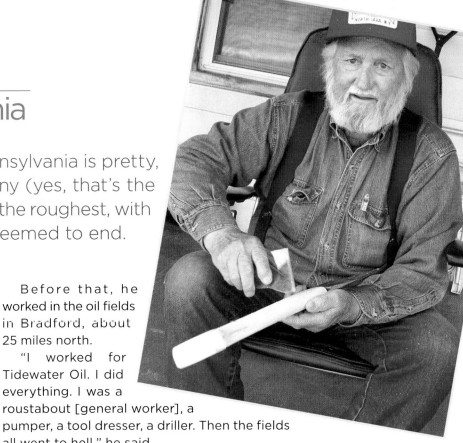

his was not a good weekend. Northern Pennsylvania is pretty, but very hilly. The stretch from Port Allegany (yes, that's the way they spell it) to Smethport was perhaps the roughest, with a series of short but steep hills that never seemed to end.

The next day, it got worse. I missed a turn at Smethport and walked five miles in the wrong direction—almost all of it up a nasty, nasty mountain road. After a number of extremely creative curses, I made my way back to the turn I should have taken.

Late in the day, I saw Ed Fox whittling an ax handle on his front porch.

"Come on over and set a spell," he called out. It didn't take any more coaxing. I had walked 18 miles—including five in the wrong direction—and was ready for a break.

So I just sat beside Ed and learned things that city guys hardly ever learn, like hickory is the best wood for ax handles.

"Hickory is the strongest wood there is," Ed said, as he whittled away. "The Amish use it for chairs and baskets and stuff like that. If you can make a pack basket [backpack] out of that, it will last forever."

Ed (Edward D. Fox—there's another Ed Fox nearby) lives outside Hazel Hurst, one of the many tiny towns in the northern Pennsylvania hills. He's been working on this ax for about two weeks, off and on.

He found the blade in the woods, cleaned it and sharpened it. Now he's nearly done with the handle. It's an impressive tool, and heavy as all get-out. It has to be heavy, because Ed uses it as a hammer when he's hunting, although he's getting a little old for hunting.

"At 84, about all I can do is whittle," he said. Oh, he still catches a wild critter every once in a while. And he still owns a little feed store next to his house. But life isn't what it used to be.

Once, Ed operated a farm and raised a family on this land while he was working for the state highway department.

Before that, he worked in the oil fields in Bradford, about 25 miles north.

"I worked for Tidewater Oil. I did everything. I was a roustabout [general worker], a pumper, a tool dresser, a driller. Then the fields all went to hell," he said.

According to Ed, some "experts" pumped water into the ground to force the oil out more quickly. It worked for a while, but soon the fields were flooded and useless.

Not everyone around here agrees with that assessment, but Ed didn't strike me as the type to worry about what others think.

In fact, the only time he seemed to have second thoughts was when I asked him about his family. He has children who live nearby, but one of his daughters died before she was 25.

Ed mentioned her. Then he stopped. He had to compose himself (curmudgeons aren't supposed to get weepy). He went on, but he didn't have the same enthusiasm.

I guess that's what losing a child does—you go on, but it's not the same.

After the walk, I talked with Ed on the phone and I told him I was writing a book. He said his health isn't so great.

"I hope I'm around to get one of them books," he said.

So do I.

Noble Riverside Inn
Cambridge Springs

You just never know how things will turn out in this life. Take the case of Dr. John Gray, who bought some property in Crawford County Pennsylvania more than a century ago, hoping to strike it rich with oil.

But the only thing oozing from his land was water. Who would have thought that it would be more valuable than oil? somehow word spread that there was magic in the water; it could cure your ailments. (It's been said that Dr. Gray had something to do with promoting that story.)

As tales of the mineral spring's healing power grew, more and more people traveled to the source. In 1885, Gray built the Riverside Inn to accommodate the pilgrims. It became one of the most famous spas in the nation, with eight trains a day bringing tourists to town.

The hotel kept its aura for decades, but the building eventually declined. Perhaps it was the faded glory that attracted Mike Halliday, a lawyer who loves to rescue things. (He rescues people too, but that's another story.)

So, when Mike tried to coax his wife, Marie, into visiting the hotel in 1985, she refused to even look at it. She knew what he had in mind. When Marie relented and visited the inn, she was horrified.

"I said, 'My God, Mike, the paint is peeling, the wallpaper's coming down, the porch is sagging. Don't even think about buying this,'" Marie recalled, as she sat in the hotel lobby.

Well, it was too late of course. Mike was already negotiating to buy the building.

Nearly 20 years later, Marie, the practical one, still spends six days (and many nights) a week greeting guests, paying bills, planning events and talking with cooks and gardeners at the sprawling wooden complex.

The first thing she did when they purchased the building was to fix the inn's 14 furnaces so the hotel could stay open in the cold weather.

Marie and Mike added weekend events, like dinner theaters, murder mysteries, wine tastings, magic shows and a Christmas gala. There's a chess tournament that celebrated its 100th year here last week, and there's an annual convention of Nelson Eddy fans. Honest.

The events, along with weddings and receptions, draw customers to the hotel and restaurant.

"On Mother's Day, we served 1,032 people," Marie said.

Mike is still a lawyer, but he helps out at the hotel. Many of the furnishings are his ideas.

"He stopped at every tag sale and antique place and came back with the strangest things," Marie said. She added that he's finally becoming the maintenance man he always thought he was.

"He walks around with this tool belt, but he doesn't know what to do with half the things in it," she chuckled.

Walk down the hall and you'll see different wallpaper, beds and furnishings in each room.

"People tell us it's like going to their grandma's house," said one longtime employee.

Unfortunately, the years have taken their toll on Marie. She says she doesn't have as much zest and energy. It might be time to hand the hotel on to a younger owner, she said. But Marie and Mike won't sell to just anybody.

"We have so much of ourselves in this—we have to find someone who will care for it as much as we do," she said.

Then she went back to work.

Penn Pals Venango

This is an old-fashioned love story: Convict writes to professor, then later they meet by chance, fall in love and live happily ever after in a church.

Just a regular old love story.

John Edwards bought the two-story church in tiny Venago more than a decade ago, and spent years renovating it. Unfortunately, the government took a dim view of his other enterprise—growing marijuana in nearby Erie.

John served two years in federal prison, where he led a literary group. At one point, he wrote to Diana Hume George, asking for her advice when the group was discussing the role of women in Shakespeare's plays. Diana is an author and professor of English and Women's Studies at The Behrend College at Penn State University at Erie.

Well, Diana's son is a cop, and he had a thing or two to say about responding to unsolicited letters from prison. So she didn't answer John.

Later, when John was free, he spotted Diana in a bookstore. He recognized her from a picture on one of her books and introduced himself. They became friends and went out together occasionally.

Then John invited Diana to his house, and she fell in love—with the former church.

"When I walked in, my jaw dropped. I've frequently been accused of marrying him for the building," Diana said, as she sat in a comfy chair nestled between two 15-foot-high stained-glass windows. There are eight more windows like it under the 24-foot ceiling.

"I feel honored to live here," Diana said. "I think of all the people who worshiped here, who were baptized here, who were married here—we're the restorers and guardians of this place."

John bought the church long after the congregation had moved out and the building was deconsecrated. His first impression was underwhelming.

"It was kind of dismal. It looked like a haunted house," he said.

I encountered the church almost by chance. The Venango villagers had gathered to meet me as I walked through their town. One of them said I should see the church and asked John if we could take a look inside. He said, "Sure."

So all of us paraded over to the church.

Poor Diana had no idea what was going on. She was reading a book when upwards of 15 neighbors and strangers walked into her living room, ready for a tour of her house. But she was a good sport, and soon we were having quite a party.

The villagers knew there was something in John's past, but they were more interested in his present. They know him as their part-time postmaster and former library-board member.

Diane sees more in him. She says John's marijuana days are far, far behind him.

"He's the kindest man I know. I've never heard him say a bad thing about anybody," she said. John has equally nice things to say about Diana.

Like I said, it's just an old-fashioned love story.

Pen pals in their converted church.

Sign Garden Meadville

When Amara Geffen plants a garden, she does it big—and unusual. Just look at her handiwork—12-foot-high daisies, chrysanthemums, daffodils and lilies of the valley in the garden that her students created west of downtown Meadville.

Now here's the unusual part: they're all made from discarded road signs.

There's a daisy with petals made out of white one-way signs that radiate from the center, which is a red stop sign. There's another daisy, made with yellow signs.

"People pull over and come back to look at the flowers. They want to buy them," said John Moyer, assistant manager at the DOT complex next to the garden. The project began after the DOT asked Allegheny College to help spruce up the property. Geffen, director of the Arts and Environment Initiative, took on the task.

First they started with real flowers, but the students wanted to do more. Amanda told them they would have to get their materials from the DOT site, which includes a highway maintenance area. One student suggested making flowers out of road signs.

The first one—the stop-sign daisy—was an instant hit with passersby. Soon the students were working with DOT road crews, welders and equipment operators to create the flowers from stop signs, one-way signs, speed-limit signs and town-name signs.

DOT workers were skeptical at first, but not for long.

"By the end of summer the guys were bringing in flowers and saying: "Can we make one like this?" Amara said.

The project worked so well that DOT asked the students to use more signs to screen their working area from the road. Now they're building a mural that depicts regional features.

Good things happen when people work together.

Left—Two artists at a highway-sign mural. Right—Friends in Meadville

Meadville Heroes

I f I could, I'd personally thank all of the people who made my journey through Meadville and Crawford County a pleasure. People greeted me on the street, walked with me, beeped as they drove by, waived from their homes and offered gifts.

Hundreds, perhaps thousands, of people welcomed Travis and me. It was beyond our expectations. I've been inspired by the kindness of people I met throughout this adventure, but in Crawford County I was overwhelmed by generosity.

Best of LucK ON your JOURNEY, JOE. KEEP TRUCKING

Saving The Big Duck
Conneaut Lake

Conneaut Lake carousel

hink of Conneaut Lake as The Little Town That Could. If the fates are kind, it will be one of the few communities in the nation to own a real amusement park.

Cynics might say the folks from Conneaut Lake are dreamers, and their plan to save a once-glorious park is a fantasy. But I'm rooting for them, just like we all cheered for the Little Engine That Could.

There's a lot to root for. These folks are trying to save one of the area's biggest attractions while at the same time preserving a piece of history and providing a summer haven for families.

At Conneaut Lake kids can ride, swim and cavort all day for just few a dollars, and old-timers can return to the past for an afternoon. Later, the whole family can unwind over a sit-down meal in the grand hotel.

That's the way it's been for a century, including the years when Conneaut Lake was a national landmark that attracted the country's top performers. All the big bands came here. Doris Day sang in the Dreamland Ballroom. Perry Como got his start here. (For those under 30: Perry Como was this old guy who was super relaxed when he sang—like Frank Sinatra. Um, Frank Sinatra was this old guy...)

"In the early 1900s it wasn't unusual for 10,000 people to come here on a Sunday," said Judith Hughes, one of the people trying to revive the park and its centerpiece, the big wooden hotel.

There are reports of ghosts there. But that's another story. Now the park is haunted by financial hobgoblins. An owner went bankrupt in the 1990s and left the park to the community. It was devastating for everyone who depended on the park for income. Folks around here call Conneaut Lake Park the Big Duck in the pond that feeds all the little ducks, like restaurants, motels and scores of summer workers.

The Board of Directors, whose members come from several nearby communities, is restoring the hotel, the rides and the grounds. The next step is to lure a steady stream of customers back to the park.

It's not Disney World, but there are 40 rides, many of them in Kiddie Land.

"We have a marvelous carousel with some of the original horses and an authentic hand organ from the 1930s," Judith said.

There are also real pony rides, a beach, a boardwalk and the Blue Streak, reportedly one of the nation's oldest roller coasters.

"When I was in high school, I rode the Blue Streak 64 times in one day," Judith said. She rode the coaster as recently as last year, but today she prefers to sit on the hotel veranda sipping a soda and looking out at the lake.

And what a bargain. You can buy a day pass for all rides for under $15 on the weekend and under $10 on weekdays. Parking and admission are free.

"Yes, it's an amusement park, but it's just, just so much more," Judith said. "It's the trees, the water. It's walking on the boardwalk in the moonlight."

I can't help but think of Lincoln Park, one of the premiere amusement areas in Massachusetts 50 years ago. All that remained when I walked past Lincoln last month were a few dilapidated buildings and the skeleton of a roller coaster.

It's enough to make you hope that Conneaut Lake really is the Little Town That Could.

Fish Story   Linesville

Lake Pymatuning is no place for the squeamish. Toss a crust of bread into the water, and watch thousands of vacant-eyed carp surge to the surface, forming an eerie carpet of wriggling bodies.

"I bet there are 10,000 of them there," said one visitor, watching the feeding frenzy near a spillway that connects two parts of the lake. Folks in Linesville say the spillway gets so thick with fish that ducks actually walk on them.

People have been feeding the big brown-and-gold carp for decades, and these fish know a free lunch when they see one.

Go ahead—toss your bread in. There's brief, fierce churning when it lands. Throw in another chunk, and more fish arrive. It's like feeding pigeons in the park. Soon the carp are packed so tightly that some of them get squeezed out of the water and wiggle on top of the pile like college kids crowd-surfing in a mosh pit.

And what a pile! The carp seem to stand upright in the water, with only their gaping mouths and dark eyes showing. It's like a scene from a Stephen King movie.

"I used to have nightmares about falling in," said a Linesville woman who never liked the spillway, but comes here anyway. It's weird, it's repulsive and it's mesmerizing.

"People are fascinated by it. You're not going to see anything like it anywhere else," said Doug Smith of Linesville. The spillway is the number-one attraction not just in Linesville, but in all of Pennsylvania's state parks, he said.

Certainly the fat, happy carp don't object. Nor do the ducks. Throw a crust into the open water and the ducks get to it first every time, proving, once and for all, that ducks are quacker than fish.

Countless carp competing for crumbs at Lake Pymatuning   **67**

OHIO

The big O at Cedar Point

Spring In The Midlands

The corn was just starting to sprout when I walked into Ohio. I watched it grow across the state. In just a few weeks, it was knee-high.

Route 6, straight and flat in Ohio, looks and feels different than the winding, tree-lined roads of the Northeast. The fields are bigger and the farmhouses are set farther back.

Even as you approach Cleveland, Euclid Avenue (Route 6) is a long, straight stretch through urban East Cleveland before it curves into downtown, where it runs just a few blocks from Lake Erie and the Rock and Roll Hall of Fame. From Cleveland to Sandusky, Route 6 follows the lakeshore, but it's still more or less a straight line.

People told me there wasn't much to see on the road from Sandusky to Fremont. I think they were wrong. There are big farms and friendly folks who invite you to stop and have a cold drink or a sandwich. Once upon a time, this was part of the Great Black Swamp: a huge chunk of uninhabited marshes and wetlands in northwestern Ohio. It took 40 years to drain the swamp, starting in the 1850s. Settlers even built a log road over the swamp to connect Fremont and Perryville, near Toledo. It was a very bumpy stagecoach ride.

West of Fremont, I encountered a wide swath of purple, white, green, yellow and red wildflowers on the roadside. Someone must have appreciated Mother Nature's handiwork because there was a sign that said "Do Not Spray or Mow."

The Birdman of Andover
Andover, Ohio

**D**on't be fooled by Jim Beckett's long, stringy hair, his scraggly goatee and tattoo-covered arms. They hide the gentle man inside.

Just watch him coax a blue-and-gold parrot out of its cage and hold it like an infant. Watch the parrot snuggle against his shoulder for protection. That's the real Jim Beckett. The real Birdman.

"I've been around birds all my life," Jim said, as a macaw perched on his forearm. Just a few months before I met him, Jim opened a pet store near Andover, Ohio.

The store is barely breaking even, but Jim isn't in it for the money. The birds and other creatures are his family. He won't sell them to just anybody. At Birdman's, you have to convince Jim you'll be a good parent.

"If you can't take care of yourself, you can't take care of a bird," he said.

The birds, fish, dogs, snakes, spiders and other critters are just part of Birdman's menagerie. There are more animals at home.

"This is what my house looks like," Jim said, pointing to a room lined with birdcages. Before he opened the store, his house was overflowing with creatures.

But when a snake escaped from its cage, Birdman's wife, LouAnn, told him it was time to open a pet store.

Actually, she was blunter than that.

"I said no more snakes in the house," she said.

LouAnn doesn't mind the other animals. She even takes care of them when Jim's busy at the store or working for the county water department.

Yes, she sees Birdman's tattoos, his hair and goatee, but she also sees the man beneath.

"He's got a big mouth, but he doesn't bite. He's very good with animals and people," she said.

Besides, she likes long hair.

Jim Beckett's gentle companion

Rock & Roll Hall of Fame
Cleveland

 **B**ack in 1967, you could get you a ticket the biggest music concert ever for seven bucks—the price of a fancy coffee and pastry today.

That concert, of course, was Woodstock, the free-love festival that was all things: the symbol of what was wrong with the next generation, the symbol of what was right with the next generation, a musical compendium never equaled, a hygienist's worst nightmare, the place were lots of babies were started, and a financial disaster for the promoters.

Not bad for seven bucks. Never mind that most of the Woodstock attendees didn't bother to buy tickets. They just came to the upstate New York town of Watkins Glen and overwhelmed the barriers that were meant to keep freeloaders out of the festival. It wasn't a very proud calling card for the next generation.

You can still get a taste of Woodstock (without the mud) at the Rock and Roll Hall of Fame in Cleveland. You can spend an entire day listening to Janis Joplin, Joan Baez, Credence Clearwater Revival or Blood, Sweat and Tears.

And a lot of things that you couldn't get at Woodstock are on display here, in the shining glass building on the edge of Lake Erie.

"I loved seeing the clothes they wore," said 22-year-old Onaliese Bailey of Guilford, Connecticut as she toured the museum. Maybe she was talking about Jimi Hendrix' psychedelic yellow, green and blue outfit which included a black-and-hot-red robe, green boots and, of course, flair pants. But that was nothing next to Mick Jagger's skin-tight pants and a cape that looks like a combination of a Union Jack and American flag.

Rock & Roll Hall of Fame entrance

Elsewhere, you can explore the 500 songs that shaped Rock and Roll, or you can find out what makes the music of Ohio unique. You can see what songs topped the charts and which ones were international hits.

The museum isn't limited to rock and roll. You'll find pre-rockers, like Frank Sinatra, as well as folk, blues and country artists. That makes sense, because so much of music is connected.

In fact, I spent most of my time at a hands-on (and ears-on) exhibit that lets you see and hear how performers influenced each other. I discovered the connection between the Beatles and the Mamas and Papas. And I heard hints of the Everly Brothers in Simon and Garfunkel.

You can even uncover connection between the Sex Pistols and Iggy and the Stooges—I passed on that one.

Ray Labbe of Brunswick, Maine liked that exhibit even more than I did. "I think it was awesome," he said. Then he told my why a 22-year-old guy would come to a museum highlighting forty-year-old music.

"If it was good back then, it will be good now."

When I was there, there was a theater with tribute to Jimi Hendrix. Inside, I chuckled at all these white-haired old folks listing to very loud music—then I realized I was one of them.

Wall of Sorrow East Cleveland

From Euclid Avenue, Cleveland's downtown buildings gleam in the distance, a bit like Oz. But Euclid Ave is in East Cleveland, a million miles from downtown's glitter. Good industrial jobs left long ago; storefronts are vacant.

Yet there's a place here that touches your soul more deeply than all the downtown glitter. It's a wall with the names of 800 Cleveland area youngsters who were killed from 1990 to 2002.

Below the names are drawings, photographs, flowers, poems, and messages from families and friends: the epitaphs of broken dreams, of promises not kept.

There's a picture of a basketball player, a girl in a prom dress, a young Marine in uniform. There's a photo of Willie Tipton Jr., his eyes glowing with confidence. Next to the picture a friend wrote, "Rest in peace, bro."

There are family portraits and a picture of Aaron McCarter, who was struck down by hit-and-run driver. He's among the 150 youths killed since 2002.

"Aaron left to mourn a host of family and friends. We love you and you will be missed dearly," says a message from his family.

Then there's another message.

"You were truly a gift from God. Love always, Your big sister, Leiliani"

They say almost no one walks by the wall without pausing for a moment. Passersby look at the mementos of people they knew. They search for new faces on the wall.

"I knew him, and him, and him," neighborhood resident Greg Morse said, pointing to each of the pictures. "This girl, they shot her in the side of the head. She was a beautiful girl. They're all gone."

"It's dangerous here. Real dangerous."

The memorial was inspired by Judy Martin, after her son was killed in 1994. Back then, it was the simple, private gesture of a grieving parent. Others who lost children followed Judy's lead, and soon there was a wall.

But that was just the beginning. Judy and community activist Art McKoy realized that the area and the nation were in the midst of an epidemic of homicides of children.

The wall has become a reminder of that epidemic, and each new picture is a call to action.

"This wall says: We will never forget. We will never let it happen again," said Art, who operates Black on Black, an organization that provides services for people in East Cleveland.

Judy and other parents talk with youngsters at schools and with families at vigils, trying to instill a respect for life. She said those talks may have something to do with the decline in child homicides in the past two years.

Which makes you wonder why the city is willing to see the wall destroyed. The wall is part of a vacant building, which East Cleveland acquired for unpaid taxes. Now the city is trying to sell the building—presumably a death sentence for the wall.

"They've been showing the building," Judy said. If it has to come down, parts of the wall could be moved. But she said grieving parents should have a place where they can leave poems, flowers and cards, or write a message next to a picture. Ideally, the spot would have a little garden where people could sit and reflect.

Judy and Art have a better idea: Use the building as a community center for young people. That would transform it into a living memorial.

NOTE: I wish I could report that things have gone well for Art and Judy, but the wall came down after I left. When the city targeted the building for demolition, Art, Judy and other local folks took it down piece-by-piece for storage.

"I'm devastated. It was a blow," Judy said, adding that some people who had placed memorials on the wall couldn't bring themselves to take them down. It was like giving up on their children.

But Judy hasn't given up. She hopes the wall will return better than ever. She wants to create a space with flowers, shrubs and benches.

Art is even more optimistic. He expects the wall to return in some form. The pictures, drawings and other memorials are being stored in several spots now.

"It left a big hole that can only be filled by putting up another wall." When Art says that, you believe it's going to happen.

Art McKoy in front of the wall

Women With Hats
Cleveland

 **W**hat do you get when you mix women in hard hats with ladies in red hats?
No, not a very bad country song.

You get a picture of American women in different places and different times.

I spotted the offices of Hard Hatted Women in a small building at the edge of downtown Cleveland, not far from the Rock and Roll Hall of Fame. I just had to walk in and find out who they were.

I met Kelly Kupcak, who told me the organization began in Cleveland 30 years ago, when three workers met to share their problems and ideas.

A construction worker's life is never easy, but it's a lot harder for women, who are outnumbered by men by about 30 to 1. They have to prove themselves time and again, Kelly said.

"It would be sad for them to leave because they didn't feel connected or supported," she said.

Hard Hatted Women helps these workers cope with the realities of the business. It offers discussion groups, educational programs and job training. Members also talk to students about the prospects of working in the trades.

"We talk to them real honestly," Kelly said. "We tell them there are times when you are unemployed."

But there also are opportunities, and women excel when they get the chance, she said.

"Absolutely, they can do it. We've seen women become foremen and supervisors."

In some ways, the Red Hatted Ladies are the opposite of the Hard Hatted Women. After all, you're more likely to find a Red Hatted Lady at a tea party than a construction site. They wear their signature bonnets to meetings and events and generally have a good, lighthearted time when they get together.

The official Red Hat Society has hundreds of chapters across the country and more throughout the world. Each chapter has a queen, and the head of the society is called the queen mother.

Here are the society's rules:

1. Wear a red hat (pink if you're under 50) and a purple dress to events.

2. Have fun.

I suspect there's a rule that you have to be female, but I attended red-hat events in Linesville, Pennsylvania, and Holdrege, Nebraska, on my journey. Heck, I was the guest of honor, and these ladies treated me with all the respect I deserved—but I had a good time anyway. I even wore a red hat that looked like a colossal escapee from the Easter Parade.

So does that make the Hard Hatted Women and the Red Hatted Ladies opposites? Not really. They're just people in different situations. They could have a lot in common. Who knows, some Hard Hatted Women might be Red Hatted Ladies when they're not working.

But I wouldn't bet on that.

A lone man does his best to ignore the Red Hatted Ladies in Linesville

Erie Shore
Lakewood to Sandusky

**W**alking out of Cleveland along Detroit Ave. and Lake Ave., I traveled from struggling city streets to suburbs with brick houses, neatly trimmed lawns, flowers and shrubs, squirrels and birds. Here, East Cleveland and Euclid Ave. are on the other side of the world.

At Rocky River on this day, Lake Erie is a patchwork of blue, green and gray fading into the morning mist offshore. There's a pocket of fishermen (and fisher-women) on the pier at Bradstreet's Landing.

"Basically, it's yellow perch right now. Next month it will be small-mouth bass," said Steven Roman, who has been working at the pier for 15 years. When the water warms up in a month or so, the perch will head for deeper, cooler spots, and the bass will move in. This year's rainy spring was a boon for fishermen, who thrive when the water's high.

"Last Sunday, we had eight people limit out," Roman said.

Lake Avenue becomes Lake Road and seems to stretch forever. The farther from Cleveland you get, the more showy and out of place the houses become.

The simple cottages of the past are being replaced by mini-mansions that shout, "Look at me!"

People here say you could buy these properties for a pittance a couple of decades ago, when the lake was polluted. It smelled bad and no one wanted to live near it.

In Huron, just east of Sandusky, local native Clark Hahn watches fields where he once played transformed into condominiums. There are still farms where the tractors plow right up to the water line, but there are fewer of them.

And there are no more rugged individualists like the late Ed Otto, who went out west in the 60s and bought a few buffalo. Over the years he built a large-scale buffalo farm less than 50 miles from Cleveland. It's such an oddity that they offer tours.

"He was a real character," Clark said. "When he was in his 80s they took his license away, so when he went anywhere, he drove his big farm tractor up and down the road."

"And you had to get out of his way, because he couldn't see," added Sue Nottke.

Sue, Clark and John Girard accompanied me though Huron and into Sandusky. They pointed out places where there were once scores of summer cottages.

"Right here was the dance hall and roller-skating rink. They came here from Cleveland and Toledo for recreation," Sue said.

Clark, who was riding a bike, exulted in spotting lake islands on an uncommonly clear day.

"I can see an island right now. Wow—you can see it so clear. It's a Canadian island called Midi. Nobody lives on it," he said peering through an opening in a clump of trees.

Like a lot of people here, Clark is convinced that Erie is a great lake.

Roots
Sandusky, Ohio

Verenna Carman's doctor told her to stay home on Sunday. Her family told her to stay home too. Instead, Verenna was at the Second Baptist Church playing the organ. She's been doing it for years, and sickness wasn't going to stop her now.

"My doctor told me to rest for five days, so I said that would be Friday, Saturday, Monday, Tuesday and Wednesday—Sunday, I'll go to church," she said.

Like Verenna, the folks at Second Baptist try a little harder. They know there are a lot of ghosts (or maybe angels) looking over their shoulders in this church that was founded by seven former slaves in 1849. By the Civil War, it was known as the First Regular Anti-Slavery Baptist Church.

"This church is built on solid rock, from slavery to now. It's an honor and a privilege to be here," congregation member Walter Welch said, standing on the church steps after services.

Today, there's a brick facade, but when you walk inside, you'll see parts of the original wooden building. It can send a shiver up your spine.

"I feel a sense of strong unity here; I'm in touch with my ancestral background," assistant pastor Deborah Marshall said.

But what really makes the Second Baptist special is its down-home friendly people.

I was just a guy in a T-shirt and shorts sitting in the back row, but most of the people (decked out in white dresses and suits) who walked by shook my hand and welcomed me to the service. That's the way they do things here.

"My wife made me come here 30 years ago; the people made me stay," associate minister Bobby Langdon said. "I felt there was a love,

a harmony, an openness. People would extend themselves, and it wasn't just on Sunday."

Marshall said she and her husband came from a larger congregation 25 years ago and quickly became family.

"There was a closeness here. We didn't know anyone, and they took us in."

The building is on the National Register of Historic Places, but it may not remain an active church much longer. The congregation purchased a 27-acre site on the outskirts of Sandusky, and the members plan to build a bigger structure where they can offer more community services.

Marshall said the church won't lose its small-town closeness and the congregation will continue maintaining the original building as a historic site.

But not everyone wants to move.

"A lot of the older parishioners, they want to stay here," she said.

And why not? They have a good thing going. I planned to stop for a short while and stayed for the entire service. The music was great and I felt at home.

I hope that Second Baptist will succeed in its expansion, but bigger isn't always better.

Oh. Was Verenna glad she came to church Sunday?

"I am, I am. I'm very happy. Coming to church keeps me strong," she said.

Amen.

Sandusky Second Baptist Church (public domain photo)

Roller Coaster Heaven
Sandusky

From the start of this trip, I promised you that I'd scare myself silly at Cedar Point, which calls itself the Roller Coaster Capital of the World. (They have 16 of them!)

Well, here I am at Cedar Point, just east of Sandusky, and I'm wondering what in the world I was thinking. I'm standing in line for the Blue Streak, a vintage wooden coaster, and listening to riders on the nearby Raptor coaster scream for their lives as they twist in six double loops.

The Blue Streak is no pushover either. Its first hill is 72 feet-high and it hits 65 miles an hour.

I can feel my heart pounding and sweat is beading on my brow—and I haven't even boarded the coaster. It's overcast and I'm praying for a downpour. Never mind that 50 million people have survived the Blue Streak, I know there's always a chance I'll be stuck in a car dangling from the very highest point. In front of me, two ten year old kids don't seem to have a care in the world. Ah, the innocence of youth.

Did I mention that I'm afraid of heights? For me, the scariest ride in an amusement park is a Ferris wheel—which of course is my wife's favorite ride. My nightmare world would be inhabited by Ferris wheels all intent on stranding me at the very top. Swinging slowly in the wind.

I survived the Blue Streak (another close call), and quickly plunged into the Cedar Creek Mine coaster, then headed for Gemini, a 125-foot high coaster. Somehow I survived again and inexplicably decided to try the Mean Streak, one of the tallest wooden coasters in the world. It's 162 feet high!

I didn't say I was smart.

Once again there's that dreaded, but seductive, clinky-clanky ride up that first hill, which—I swear—went straight through the clouds. I couldn't say for sure because my eyes were closed.

I was riding with Bill McIlrath of Connecticut, a Cedar Point veteran, but even he was looking straight down at the floor as we reached the top.

Then it was swoosh! Down and fast, leaving your innards about three feet above the rest of your body. The coaster swung around doubled back, bringing us through tunnels of wooden staging and under tracks we'd already conquered. It was a great ride.

Did I mention that I love wooden coasters? And I conquered them all at Cedar Point.

(No one needs to know that even the Mean Streak is small compared to the park's newest ride, the Top Thrill Dragster, a metal coaster which rises 420 feet and hits speeds of up 120 miles an hour. There's nothing on earth that could get me onto that contraption.)

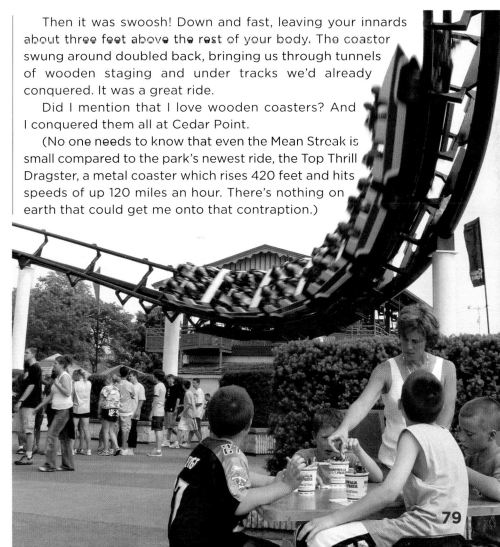

Cedar Point coasters

War & Peace at Put-In-Bay
Middle Bass Island

In a tribute to both war and peace, the Perry's Victory and International Peace Memorial, overlooks Lake Erie just a stone's throw from Sandusky.

You didn't know that? My goodness, where were you when the rest of us were learning Commodore Oliver Perry's trademark phrase "We have met the enemy and they are ours" in the War of 1812—not to be confused with Pogo's immortal "We have met the enemy and he is us."

The memorial's centerpiece is a 352-foot-tall monument on Middle Bass, one of five major islands near Sandusky. It towers over Put-in-Bay, where Perry's ragtag navy defeated an equally ragtag collection of British ships, giving the Americans control of Lake Erie.

Just about every local college student is familiar with Put-in-Bay. Unfortunately it's not because they know their history. Put-in-Bay Village is where young folks go revel, which is a fancy word for getting drunk. It's sort of an all-summer spring-break spot, with attractions like the alleged longest bar in the world.

The reveling is mostly at night. During the day Put-in-Bay is a family-friendly tourist town with sightseeing trams and such. The rest of the island is dotted with summer homes.

I took the ferry to Middle Bass to visit the memorial, not to revel. Honest.

It was worth the trip. Stand on the monument's 317-foot high observation deck, and you can see all five islands—Middle Bass, South Bass, North Bass, Kelly's Island and Pelee Island, which is actually in Canada. On a clear day you can see the Canadian mainland. You'll also be standing 12 feet higher than the Statue of Liberty's torch, but who's counting. And, yes, there is an elevator.

I met Don Hart who was returning to the monument with his family. Don had taken his kids to the monument when they were young, and this was sort of a goodbye trip for his son John, who was scheduled to head to Kosovo with the Army National Guard. John thought his military

obligation was over, but the service called him back—and no, his family doesn't think it's fair.

The monument is an appropriate site for a military departure. Commodore Perry's victory gained control of Lake Erie, which in turn helped America recapture Detroit. The war paved the way for treaties that would eventually create a U.S.-Canadian border without forts or warships, which is why it's also a peace memorial.

For the record, this is just one of several peace sites along the national border, including the world's first international peace park at Waterton-Glacier Park in Montana and Alberta.

If you're touring Middle Bass Island by boat, you'll notice a ship sticking out of a high cliff. I nearly spent a night on that boat, but plans fell through at the last moment, and I had to settle for a visit the next day.

The ship is part of a 194-ton lake freighter, which was the flagship of Henry Ford's fleet of oar-carrying boats. It was originally named the Benson Ford, after one of Henry's sons.

The 50-foot-high boathouse includes the captain's quarters, an office, a lounge, an officer's mess, a pilot house and the state rooms where Ford entertained his guests. Stand on the bow, which stretches out over a cove, and you'll feel like you're on the water.

How did the boat get up there? With great difficulty, including battles with a neighbor and local authorities for approval. The boat is now owned by Cleveland auto dealer Bryan Kasper, who purchased it at an auction.

I wonder what Perry would have thought if he had seen Kasper's boat sticking out from a cliff.

Left—Put-in-Bay and (inset) the war and peace memorial / Above—The freighter Benson Ford on a cliff

Ketchup
Freemont

The farms of northern Ohio are wonderful in late spring. Fields of light-green soy beans. Neat rows of young corn pushing through the dark soil.

On a gusty day, you'll see birds trying to fly against the wind only to be blown backward before giving up.

East of Fremont, I noticed a strange aroma. It had a spicy tomato scent, but I didn't see anything that would produce the smell. It came and went, but grew stronger as I walked west. It made my mouth water and my taste buds lust for French fries. But where the heck was it coming from?

Then, on the edge of Fremont, I approached a tall smokestack with the number 57 on it. I was smelling Heinz ketchup.

I don't know what Heinz puts in its ketchup, but corn syrup is definitely one ingredient. There were 29 black, round railroad tankers waiting in line to deliver corn syrup to the plant.

As you reach western Ohio, the fields get bigger, stretching perhaps two miles back from Route 6. Corn that was just sprouting a week or two ago is now knee high—although my knees aren't very high.

There are a lot more dead birds by the roadside out here. I'm told it's because the birds fly low over the roadway, hopping from cornstalk to cornstalk rather than from tree to tree.

I paused to sniff some yellow and red flowers east of Napoleon. The scent was delicious, but I left quickly after an unpleasant encounter. So now I have a warning:

On life's journey, take time to stop to smell a rose.
But beware of bees that might sting your nose.

Rutherford B. Hayes
Freemont

 n Colonial times, Ohio was considered the Far West. The kind of place where Daniel Boone blazed trails. In fact, there's monument in Fremont, where Boone was captured by Indians in the 1760s.

Ohio was still considered the West a century later, when Rutherford B. Hayes moved to Spiegel Grove, the estate in Fremont once owned by his grandfather.

Hayes was a general, a governor and the 19th U.S. President, but it's Hayes' humanity that impresses Nancy Kleinhenz, communications manager for the Hayes Presidential center in Fremont. He was a voice for the newly freed slaves and for the Native Americans. And he worked hard to heal the nation's wounds after the Civil War, she said.

"He was a genuine good guy. He came into office after the corruption of the Grant administration and tried to change things," Nancy said.

When Hayes was starting out as an attorney, his first client was a black man accused of murder.

"It was risky, but he always acted with his heart," she said.

Although he was a successful lawyer in Sandusky by the 1860s, Hayes volunteered for service in the Civil War and rose to the rank of major general. He was wounded four times, at least once seriously.

Hayes was elected to the U. S. House in

1864, even though he refused to campaign while in the army. He was later elected governor for three terms before running for president in 1876. The election was so close that a special commission was appointed to rule on disputed votes.

Hayes left many legacies, including civil-service reform and a law allowing women lawyers to appear before the Supreme Court. His integrity helped restore the image of the president after the corruption and cronyism of the Grant administration.

He was the first president to use the phone and the typewriter in the White House. His wife, Lucy, was the first presidential spouse to graduate from college and the first to be called First Lady.

What's Hayes' most enduring legacy? He started the Easter-egg rolling tradition in 1878.

He died at Spiegel Grove January 17, 1893, and he's buried on the grounds.

Unlike other presidential museums, Spiegel Grove is a combination library, presidential home and archive. There's even a footpath along the river that Daniel Boone used back when Ohio was the Far West.

Spiegel Grove

A Green Town
Bowling Green

Bowling Green is a college town just north of Route 6. It started as a tiny settlement in the Great Black Swamp and thrived in the 1800s when folks found natural-gas deposits here. It's also farm country.

Maybe that's why Bowling Green is so conscious of the environment. After all, this is the place where homeowners asked the city to put a 390-foot-high windmill in their backyard. Well it's actually at the landfill, but you can see it from most everywhere in this flat country. In fact, it's become a local attraction. People are always stopping at the landfill to see the oddity up close.

Where I come from in Connecticut, towers like that are built only after the neighbors howl and sue—if they're built at all. But when the idea for a giant wind turbine came up here, the city asked electric users if they would be willing to spend more for green energy. Enough people said yes to make the project worthwhile.

"We're a university town. People here are interested in the environment and in emissions," said Daryl Stockburger, the city's Director of Utilities.

There was only one turbine when I visited the site, but Stockburger said the project is so popular that two more are on the way. It will be Ohio's first real wind farm, generating electricity for several thousand homes.

If you're looking for raw power in Bowling Green, try the National Tractor Pulling Championships every August. And if you want brain power, there's Bowling Green State University and the annual Black Swamp Art Festival.

Not far from the turbines, a sheriff stopped me on a busy four-lane section of Route 6 that might well have been off limits to pedestrians. I expected a lecture or maybe even a summons.

Instead the lawman handed me $5 and wished me well on my journey.

That's the kind of power I like—the power of a simple act of kindness.

Bowling Green's wind turbine dwarfs two cars

High Court
Napoleon, Ohio

T he Court House in Napoleon is a huge brick, wood and limestone building that towers over its neighbors.

There's a balcony and steeple like turrets atop the court—and a 15-foot high statue of the Goddess of Justice above the bell tower. Inside, the ceilings are at least a dozen feet high.

You have to wonder how little Napoleon wound up with this impressive building. It's hard to believe the county needed such a big court in 1882.

But I'm told Napoleon was a prosperous town back then. An ice-age lake once covered the area, leaving behind the Great Black Swamp that stretched more than 100 miles east and west. The nasty muck and mosquitoes kept settlers away until the 1800s.

But when the swamp was drained it left ideal farmland. The Maumee River and the Miami-Erie Canal drew farmers and merchants to Napoleon, making it a thriving market center. That's how Napoleon could afford a grand building—at the staggering cost of $95,000.

By the way, there's a nearby Indiana town called Waterloo. Sports headline writers must love it when Napoleon plays Waterloo.

"Napoleon Gets Revenge At Waterloo" or perhaps "Napoleon Beaten At Waterloo—Again.

Napoleon's court house dominates the town's center

INDIANA

For God & Country

Traveling across Indiana is a journey through cultures, from the farmlands of the east to the Bible Belt and Amish country near Nappanee, to gritty Gary and the Chicago suburbs. Near Nappanee, the heart of the mobile-home industry, Route 6 has more than its share of tractor-trailers and wide loads, but in Shipshewana, the heart of Mennonite country, horse-drawn carriages and bicycles are as common as cars.

In Indiana, Route 6 runs beneath the great peninsula of Michigan, leaving Lake Erie behind. The roads here are ruler-straight, like those in Ohio, but the corn fields are bigger and the farmhouses even farther back, perhaps a half mile from the highway.

Because the land is flat I could see storm clouds approaching far in the distance—a new experience for someone from New England, where the weather pops up over the hill like an unexpected guest. I learned the hard way that even in Indiana you can't outrun the weather—those clouds are a lot faster than they look.

When I reached Gary, the Michigan peninsula was behind me, and I was just a few miles from the tip of Lake Michigan as it dips south like a giant teardrop. The lakeshore here is an odd sight, with sandy beaches stretching out beneath the smokestacks of massive steel mills.

Left—Farm fields and trucks on Route 6
Right—A steel plant on Lake Michigan

Windmills of America
Kendallville

 nce upon a time, just about every farm on the Great Plains had a windmill—or two or three. People like Russell Baker will tell you that windmills made the Midwest the breadbasket of America.

"There were hundreds of thousands of fertile acres that weren't worth anything because they couldn't get water," said Baker, manager of the Mid-America Windmill Museum in Kendallville, Indiana.

With windmills, farmers could pump underground water to irrigate their crops. Farming communities sprouted, and these towns made it profitable to build railroads throughout the Midwest.

A century ago, there were nearly 100 windmill manufacturers within 80 miles of Kendallville. But that was before electric motors could do the same job more reliably. By the 1980s, windmills seemed like part of America's past, not its future.

Now, windmills are cool again. Actually, they're called wind turbines today, and the old farm windmills look like toothpicks compared to these 30-story-high giants.

The first large-scale project began at Altamont Pass, California in the early 1980s; now they're sprouting across the country. I saw dozens of them rising like overgrown trees on the Moosic Mountains near Scranton, Pennsylvania. I saw them in Nevada and, of course, in California, where more than 4,000 turbines stretch across the Tehachapi Mountains not far from Route 6. In Bowling Green, Ohio, folks actually asked the city to build a turbine in their neighborhood.

And in Kendallville you can find dozens of windmills at the Mid-America museum. The venture is Baker's brainchild, and the

Mid-America Windmill Museum

local development corporation sponsored the project as a tourist attraction.

Baker has been running the museum since the doors opened in 1996. When I asked how many windmills they had back then, he gave me a sheepish look and said, "I think we had four."

Now there are more than two dozen spread along a walkway that winds maybe a mile from the museum's main building, and another two dozen are being restored in the warehouse.

Stroll along the path and you'll encounter a Dutch-style mill with big arms like the monsters that battled Don Quixote. Others are more traditional, with rotating wheels like those you see on most farms. There's an 1870s Raymond Sectional, which is an array of bowl-shaped fans hung sideways. Advertisements said it was cyclone-proof.

There are windmills on the ground, next to ponds, on pedestals and on top of buildings.

There's the Currie poorman's windmill that sold for $17.25 in 1933.

About 8,000 people visit the museum each year; even former Supreme Court Justice Sandra Day O'Connor walked along the path in 2004 during the town's spring windmill festival.

Maybe she was trying to figure out how to harness all that wind in Washington.

Storm Clouds
West of Kendallville

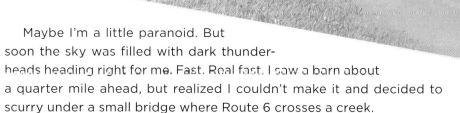

In New England we say: If you don't like the weather, wait a minute, it will change. It's different in the Midwest—the weather changes faster.

Here, I carry sunscreen and raincoat, no matter what it looks like in the morning.

Here's what happened on one "typical" Indiana day. It was beautiful at 8:30. By 10:30, a few clouds were rolling in. They were the scouts for an army of nasty relatives somewhere over the horizon.

Those first clouds were saying something like, "Scouts to leader: We've spotted Hurley. Veer six degrees southeast. Lightning bolts, prepare to fire at will."

Maybe I'm a little paranoid. But soon the sky was filled with dark thunderheads heading right for me. Fast. Real fast. I saw a barn about a quarter mile ahead, but realized I couldn't make it and decided to scurry under a small bridge where Route 6 crosses a creek.

I wasn't lonely. There were lots of birds flying around like crazy under the bridge. There were other critters too, with glowing eyes peering out from dark spots. But let's not get into that.

The rain got so heavy that I had to move deeper under the bridge. It was a pleasant break and I was safe from the storm—until lightening struck. I saw the yellow bolt hit near the riverbank, and the thunder came instantly. It sounded like a pistol fired about three inches from my ear.

That was as close as I ever want to get to untamed electricity. I moved as far under the bridge as I could, keeping one eye out for lightening and the other for critters.

Soon the rain let up and the thunder was a distant growl. I waited a few more minutes and left. When I emerged, it was sunny over my left shoulder and dark clouds hovered over my right shoulder.

After one of these storms, you can walk past a field of corn up to its ears in water, and the field across the street will be dry.

It was cooler, so I didn't put on a second round of sunscreen. By day's end, I had a sunburn. When I arrived at the hotel, it started raining again. A heavy downpour.

I no longer think Dorothy was pretty foolish for getting caught in that tornado. In the Midwest, weather travels at lightening speed.

Big Daddy
Wawaka

People who say there's no free lunch haven't been to Wawaka, Indiana, where lunch is always free at Big Daddy Merrill Frick's place.

Merrill owns Frick Services, a small company that sells farm products. About noon, 20 or so workers gather in the dining room and sit at a long table with Merrill at the head. They eat home style meals off china plates as they kid each other and tell tall tales. When a local farmer drops by at noon, they just put out another plate.

If you don't like what cook Sandy Lash puts on the table, tough luck. Eat it anyway.

"It's like I'm cooking for my family," Sandy said. If it's your birthday, she'll bake a cake and folks will sing "Happy Birthday."

Just like lunch where you work, right?

Merrill started the lunches 20 years ago because there are no restaurants in tiny Wawaka. It just didn't seem right that his folks had to drive to neighboring towns to get a meal.

Merrill's wife began making burgers, but with so many people showing up, it became a time-consuming job. So Merrill hired a cook who prepares full-course meals.

By now you've guessed that Merrill is an old-fashioned owner who thinks of his workers as family. When I met him (at lunch, of course), Merrill reminded me of Big Daddy Pollitt in Tennessee Williams' *Cat on a Hot Tin Roof.* He doesn't call himself Big Daddy, of course, but there's no doubt about who's in charge here, and Merrill knows he's a father figure.

In fact, he seemed surprised when I asked him how much the lunches cost him. "I've never thought about that," he said. It isn't about money.

Big Daddy is a testament to a time when workers weren't as disposable as tissue paper. He doesn't believe in layoffs. If you work at Frick Services, he'll find something for you to do even when business isn't so good.

Apparently, the folks in Wawaka like Big Daddy's style. Most of his employees have been there at least a decade, and some, a lot longer. There must be more to it than a free lunch.

Merlin
Nappanee

Like many Americans, Merlin Mullet wants to start his own business. But Merlin isn't looking for a better job; he's connecting with his roots.

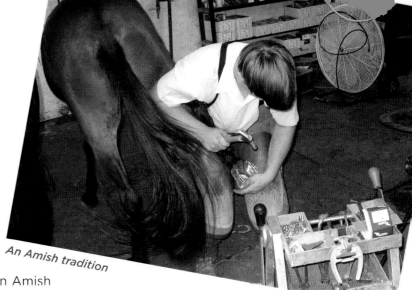

An Amish tradition

For him, working at home and living a simple life is an article of faith. He's Amish.

For generations, the Amish lived in farming communities apart from American society. Now, their way of life is threatened by success. The Amish, or Plain People, have large families and most of their children choose the Amish way. But you can divide a farm only so many times before it becomes too small to support a family.

In northern Indiana, the land crunch hit during Merlin's generation. His grandfather was a farmer. His dad was a farmer at first, but eventually took a paying job. These days, many Amish work in mobile-home manufacturing businesses in Nappanee, about midway across the state on Route 6.

"They're great workers," said Nappanee Mayor Larry Thompson. The industry pays well, and money that the Amish earn goes back into the community, Larry said.

But Merlin worries that the money and the outside lifestyle are leading people away from their beliefs.

"When they started taking jobs in the factories, my grandpa said that was the beginning of the end for us. I think he might have been right."

That's why Merlin and his wife, Mary Lou, began a family-style restaurant in a converted barn just a few months before we met them. They want to get back to the old ways, to their roots.

"I know I'm not going to be able to farm. My main goal is to be at home with my family," Merlin said.

The Amish believe that their world should revolve around Christ. Clothing fashions, lavish possessions and other worldly attractions are distractions.

Here's an Amish joke. A family is leaving a Sunday service and the man proudly says to his wife, "I do believe we were the plainest people there."

You get the point. The fancy clothes aren't the problem, it's the attitudes they create.

Working in the factories isn't the problem, either, it's the attitude it creates. Merlin can see it in his generation. He fears that some of his contemporaries like their new lives in the shops and their big paychecks.

"It's not the work; it's the possessions that go with it. People get more independent. They say 'I don't need you.' That's not the Christian way, I think. From a Christian point of view, you should want to help others."

"We don't help build each others' houses as much as we did. We go get someone to do it."

Merlin thinks he can leave the shop in two or three years because business is good at the restaurant. Mary Lou does the cooking and she does it well. I know because I ate there. My only complaint was that I was full before the dessert arrived.

You can get a taste—literally—of the Amish life in Nappanee, the first Amish settlement in Indiana. The community started with four brothers who moved here from Ohio in 1839. Now their farm is the home of Amish Acres, a major attraction that includes farm tours, a restaurant, a theater and inn.

Take the farm tour, then settle in for a thresher's meal—the hearty family-style dinner served to the workers during harvest. Don't forget the shoo-fly pie.

Double-Wides & Narrow Roads
Nappanee

There isn't a more dangerous stretch of Route 6 than the area around Nappanee, the capital of the mobile home industry. The highway here is a two-lane road with no pedestrian space and trucks hauling those double-wides rumble along all day. If you're on any part of the road when they go by—splat!

It nearly happened to me. I was walking with the traffic when I heard a horn and looked back. The trailer was so close I had to leap off the road. Boys and girls, listen to your mother when she tells you to walk facing the traffic.

I avoided being one of the many Route 6 fatalities in Indiana. There are, perhaps, more roadside crosses here than in any other state on Route 6. I think the drainage ditches that run alongside the highways have something to do with it. If you drive off the road, you'll hit the ditch and flip.

The memorials are always touching. There's a wood cross in Nappanee for a woman named Connie that says, "No farewell words were spoken, no time to say goodbye, you're gone before we know it, and only God knows why."

And another in Syracuse with the words, "Only God loved you better than we—mom, dad and dad Nelson."

You can't pass these crosses without stopping a moment to mourn the losses.

Black Pine Albion

It's easy to like Coby when he looks up at you with those big brown eyes and holds out his hands as if to say: Come play with me. But you might want to think twice before reaching out. When he was five, Coby picked up a refrigerator and tossed it across the kitchen.

That's when his owner realized that a chimpanzee might not make an ideal pet. Who knows why the owner got a chimp in the first place. Perhaps he thought Coby would grow up to be a little boy. More likely, he didn't think at all.

It happens all the time: people buy animals, and they're shocked when they act like animals. Then they get rid of them.

Coby was one of the lucky ones. He wound up at Black Pine Animal Park in Albion, a preserve and zoo where stray and unwanted animals are the stars.

Black Pine is home to camels, emus, lions, tigers, bobcats, bears, turtles, ostriches, chimps and leopards. Some of them were born here. Others are retired circus performers. But most are human rejects.

"We get calls all the time," said Connie Hawkins, the park superintendent and senior keeper. Of course, the park takes only a few animals at a time. You can guess what happens to the rest.

"Nala (one of the park's lions) was someone's pet until she was about four months old. She was playing and someone got scratched. They wanted to put her down," Connie said. She can't imagine why people would want these animals in their homes—if they knew anything about animals.

"Every single bobcat we have was a pet. They're very aggressive, and they're smelly. We have five; we could have 50."

The park could have 100 iguanas, or maybe even a thousand.

"They're so cute in the pet store when they're this big," Connie said, putting her thumb and index finger a few inches apart. "But when they're two foot long, they can break your arm with their tail—and they grow to six feet long. The pet stores don't tell you that."

It's easy to forget just how dangerous these animals can be. Just watch Thui, an African leopard, playing with water from a hose—slapping it with his paw and biting at it as though it were a string. He looks like nothing more than a big house cat cooling off on a hot day.

But even the park's staff doesn't go into the cages with leopards. They're short-tempered and unpredictable creatures.

Coby, the chimp, poses a different problem. He's smart.

Before Coby arrived at Black Pine, he watched from his cage as a worker repaired a generator. When the job was done, the worker left his keys on a table far away from the cage.

Coby made a tool to snare the keys, and over-night took apart the generator and laid the pieces—in order—on the floor.

"We have to be careful about what we give him. He's very good at using tools, and he's very calculating," Connie said.

Linda Kratzat, a volunteer, is working with Coby on sign language.

"He knows the signs for his favorite foods and drinks. Now we're working on milk and soap bubbles," Linda said.

The problem is that there's so much to do at the park that Linda has only a few hours a week with Coby.

Maybe some of those people who think wild animals would be neat pets should volunteer at the park.

Top right to bottom left—Connie Hawkins feeds a baboon; even tigers get a treat; a black panther plays with water. **93**

Amish & Mennonites
Shipshewana

If you live in the Amish areas of northern Indiana, tourists will ask you lots of questions, such as: What are the Amish like? Why do they dress that way and ride in buggies? Can we take pictures of them?

Sometimes you'll hear more sophisticated questions, like: What's the difference between the Amish and the Mennonites?

Here are the answers (from someone who learned all he knows about the subject in the past few days).

1. They're regular, religious people.

2-3. They believe in a simple life uncomplicated by fashion. Each community decides what is appropriate. For example, some communities allow their members to have tractors, while others don't. And some allow only certain types of tractors.

4. Photos? Only if you're very careful not to take pictures of their faces. They consider that a graven image. It's best to ask first.

5. I can't answer the hard questions. (Just like in school.)

My responses come with a no-money-back guarantee. If you want a more reliable source, visit the Menno-Hof, the Mennonite-Amish center in Shipshewana, right in the heart of Indiana Amish country.

Folks in Shipshewana were besieged with questions about the Amish and Mennonites, and the visitors didn't always get the right answers. That led to the creation of the center.

"One of the Menno-Hof founders said, 'There has to be a good way to answer these questions,'" a tour guide told me.

The center makes it fun to learn about the Mennonites and Amish. At the Menno-Hof, you'll find out why so many Amish men, women and children ride bicycles and why there are so many horse-drawn buggies in the streets. There's even a simulated tornado—and that's as close to Disney World as you're likely to get in Amish country.

The Mennonites took their name from Menno Simons, a former Catholic priest who joined the Anabaptist movement, which believed that people should be baptized as adults. The Mennonites also believed in nonviolence and in a simple life. Back in the 1500s, people were killed for having such radical beliefs.

More than 30,000 people a year visit the Menno-Hof, many of them Amish, who have their own story to tell. The Mennonites weren't simple enough for Jacob Amman and his followers, the Amish. They broke with the Mennonites in the 1690s.

In nearby Waterloo, I stayed at a bed-and-breakfast run by Candi Surber, a former Mennonite. Candi is now a Methodist lay speaker, but she said her Mennonite upbringing remains with her. She believes in nonviolence and lives a relatively simple life with religion at its core. She asked us to pray with her as Travis and I left to continue our journey. And she said that's not unusual in northern Indiana.

"Religion is pretty strong here. This is the northern Bible Belt," she said.

Red, White & Purple
Walkerton, Indiana

 Sometimes, we don't know how much our lives touch others. Certainly, Carla Cain didn't realize how many people were watching when she planted a flag-shaped flower garden in front of her house in the spring of 2002. It was a personal 9-11 memorial. She didn't know it was landmark—until she planted something else the next year.

"I had 400-500 people ask me what happened to the flag," Carla said as she stood on the front porch of her house on a busy section of Route 6, about 15 miles south of South Bend.

Even though it's a two-lane road here, Route 6 is a major artery for truckers avoiding the tolls on I-80. The truckers slow down as they pass Carla's house in the village. They were among the first to notice the flag was gone.

"The truckers would stop and yell, 'Where's your flag?'"

So now, Carla is sowing another flower flag. She laid out the grid in April, then planted 285 red, white and purple petunias. She added a yellow ribbon of flowers and a blue star banner, which honors service members on active duty away from home.

"We're a military family. My son has 11 friends in the military, six of them in Iraq. I have a son-in-law in the service. My son, my daughter and my husband were all in the service," she said.

Carla invested $250 for materials—money she saved by using coupons and discounts at the supermarket. Now she and her son, Edward, do the backbreaking work of weeding and maintaining the flower beds.

It's not easy when you're 50.

"The hard part is getting back up off the ground," she said.

But it's worth it.

"If I'm out there working on it, someone will comment. People will stop and take pictures. Truckers will give me a thumbs-up," she said.

That's just about right for someone with a red-white-and-blue thumb.

Carla Cain and her son work on their flower memorial

National Lakeshore

Lake Michigan, Gary to Michigan City

The sand at Indiana Dunes National Lakeshore is so soft that it feels like you're walking on powdered silk.

"I've been to Hawaii and Florida; I've never seen sand this fine," Dorsey Bourque said when he urged me to visit the beach.

He said it's called singing sand, because it makes a sound when you walk on it.

Other than Dorsey, I couldn't find anyone who'd actually heard it sing, but one woman told me that you have to walk on it just the right way in just the right spot to hear the celestial sound.

Apparently I never hit the right spot. The sand didn't sing for me, it just grabbed me by he legs and tried to drag me down to the center of the Earth.

OK, that's a slight exaggeration. But this is a true story: I was walking along the lakeshore near a stream that meandered through the beach on its way to the lake. Suddenly, my left foot sank, ankle deep, into the wet sand. I stepped forward, and the right foot sank even deeper.

I stepped again and sank still deeper.

Quicksand. That was the thought that jumped into my mind.

Now I was scared. I stepped faster. Then I got on my hands and knees and crawled out of the quicksand.

My shoes and socks were filled with sand. I felt lucky to survive.

Later, I asked a park ranger what had happened. She said I probably stepped in an area with a high water table.

Then, with a wry smile, she assured me no one has ever drowned in the sand here.

Everyone's a comedian.

Even without the singing sands, the national lakeshore is impressive. It stretches 18 miles along Lake Michigan with 15,000 acres of beaches, dunes, swamps, bogs, a historic farm and good old Mount Baldy, a 120-foot-high dune rising up on the eastern end of the protected area.

I toured Pinhook Bog (which is actually quite a distance from the lake) with a ranger, who showed me how plants survive in a spot that's too acidic for most living creatures. She told me stories of fugitives who fled into the bog knowing no one would pursue them far into this land of murky water and uncertain soil. No one knows if the fugitives ever made it back out.

It's a lot easier today—visitors cross the tricky spots on pontoon walkways.

Chellberg Farm is also part of the lakeshore preserve. On Sundays, the volunteers dress in period costumes as they go about the chores of a farm family of more than a century ago. I met volunteer Alice Garba, who was tending a vegetable patch downhill from the original farmhouse.

Alice plants veggies that were suitable for a farm in the late 1800s: peas, brown Dutch beans, Fisher soup beans, black-Valentine string beans.

"They planted a lot of beans because they last all winter," she said. By winter's end people were eating a lot of beans.

"They can get pretty boring, so you want a mixture," she said.

Alice isn't quite sure why she does this backbreaking labor in her retirement years.

"I'm a country girl at heart," she said.

But Alice, a former teacher, also does it for the school groups that visit the farm.

"The children today have no idea what it takes to put food on the table," she said.

Ridge Road in Gary

Gary
Indiana

 group of folks joined me on the road in western Indiana, but they all left before we reached Gary, which they called the murder capital of the country. Yes, that made me nervous. But the people in Gary weren't scary, they were inspirational.

You don't hear anyone talk about Gary's history as a blue-collar steel town or the Lake Street shopping district with its boutiques, restaurants and galleries.

Maybe that's because Gary will always be overshadowed by its famous neighbor, Chicago. Just 25 miles from the Loop and the Miracle Mile, Gary is close enough to be a Chicago suburb—if Chicago would take it. And it's young enough to be the Windy City's little sister. In fact, Gary is the nation's youngest major city—born in 1906, when U.S. Steel built its plants near the lakeshore. It's a city built on steel.

The struggles of the steel industry contributed mightily to Gary's decline in the past half century, leading to a chorus of skepticism about the city's future.

But the skeptics never met Clara Blackmon and Sherecka Davis, two Gary natives who believe in the city.

Clara is principal at Ambassador Academy, an oasis of three buildings on Ridge Road, where boarded doors, broken windows and abandoned buildings are commonplace.

Clara could be working in a suburban school system, but she says she belongs at this church-run complex, helping city children. The academy must be doing something right. It started with three students seven years ago, now it has 300 from preschool to seventh grade.

"We're growing because parents are looking for a great education for their children," Clara said. "We have kindergarten students who are reading above the first-grade level."

The formula: parents, teachers and administrators are all on the same team. When students leave for the summer they have work to do before they return in the fall—and it gets done, Clara said.

"Contrary to popular belief, parents in the inner city want their children to learn. Here, they have to be involved and committed," she said.

That's why she bristles when people mock Gary.

"I'm offended because I know the talent Gary produces. There are people here who are positive, productive," she said.

Maybe she was thinking of Sherecka Davis, who teaches third grade at the academy, writes poetry and lives in Gary by choice.

"I see Gary like a phoenix. It will rise from the ashes," Sherecka said. "My husband and I want to stay in Gary, we just bought a home here."

She knows the statistics: Gary has more murders per capita than any other city in the U.S. But she also knows that statistics don't tell the whole story. She's lived in Gary her entire life and never had a problem.

Sure, there are sections of Gary she wouldn't walk through at night. But she said there are areas like that in any big city.

"There are more murders in Chicago, in New York and other cities than in Gary," she said. That's true. Gary holds the per-capita title, partly because it just barely makes the 100,000 population cutoff for the murder report. Smaller numbers make for higher percentages.

I met Sherecka during the last week of the school year, a time when many teachers are burned out. But she was still enthusiastic.

"A good day is when they're using the skills I've taught them, not because I've provoked them, but because it's now part of them," she said. "When I see that, I know I've made a difference."

And maybe she makes a difference by just staying in Gary.

City of Steel
Gary

**R**ight next to the Indiana Dunes National Lakeshore, giant mills still produce steel. You can see the smoke rising from the stacks and smell the slag as you drive by. The mills are surviving, but the city they created is struggling.

Decades ago, the steel plants were Gary's lifeblood. More than 25,000 people worked at U.S. Steel and more than 100,000 owed their livelihood to the steel industry in some way.

Today there are only about 7,000 steel workers here.

People here say that Gary is the only large U.S. city born in the 20th Century.

"They built a mill here in 1906, and the city grew up around it," said Gene Coleman, a veteran steelworker who lives in nearby Hobart.

The mills along the lakeshore are still the greatest concentration of steel manufacturing in the world, Gene said, adding that employment has dropped, but production has actually increased.

Sounds like a lot of businesses these days.

A Solider's Tale
Munster

dam Kirschner tells war stories in a light-hearted voice that makes you wonder if he's forgotten the pain. He'll talk of the mix-ups and misadventures as though they were a joke.

He hasn't forgotten, of course. The pain is right below the surface. Ask him how he really feels, and he'll tell you about the wounds he suffered, the months in the hospital and years of recovery.

"Hell no, there was nothing funny about it," he said, when I met him in Munster, Ind., just east of Gary and south of Chicago.

Adam was one of the 100 World War II veterans sent to France to represent servicemen at the international com-memoration of D-Day in 2004.

He shook hands with President Bush and other bigwigs. But Adam doesn't know why he was picked. The military says the 100 soldiers were chosen randomly.

"There were a hundred guys there who asked, 'Why me,'" he said. It was the same question many of them asked when they returned home alive while so many others perished.

Adam was a combat engineer who

landed at Omaha Beach and fought along the French coast.

He remembers riding on the beach and watching the work details gathering truckloads of body parts, trying to put them together as best they could.

The memories returned, as painful as a wound that never heals: the sights on that beach, the sounds and, mostly, the smell of death.

That's when Adam let out a big "eeeoww," as though he'd been stabbed. The memories were too much.

He couldn't speak for a moment. Then he gathered himself, but he'd said all he wanted to say—except for a final thought.

We never should have gotten mixed up in Iraq, he said.

I have just two words for Adam.

Thank you.

And that goes to everyone who puts their lives on the line for us.

Adam Kirschner with his medals

ILLINOIS

Bike path along the Hennepin Canal

Let's Shoot The Water Towers

In Illinois, Route 6 travels from Chicago-land to the mighty Mississippi—from the Midwest's big city to America's big river. Between the city and the river,

I found more American icons: cowboys, Indians, canals and the green grass of suburbia.

Mad Mac McAvoy awaited me at the Illinois border. Mac is a state transportation department legend who walked across Illinois on a bet. He guided me through Chicagoland suburbs and gave me his personal survival kit, including plastic trash bags, which he used as emergency raincoats. I tried a trash bag in a storm. They're ok, if you don't mind rivers of water running down your back.

In Chicago's suburbs, Route 6 travels through communities like Oak Forest and Oakland Park with their wide sidewalks, big modern hotels and malls. There's a lot of green here too, mostly in the form of mani-

Chicago's Navy Pier

cured lawns and neatly landscaped parks. The suburbs have spread all the way out to Joliet—about 40 miles from Chicago—and they're still growing.

The stretch between Joliet and Morris seemed to last forever. I think it was because of the water towers in Morris. I saw them and figured I was close to town. But the towers were a lot bigger than I thought—you can see them from far, far away. Danged water towers.

On the western side of the state, Route 6 parallels the old Hennepin Canal, an ill-timed attempt to link the Great Lakes with the Mississippi River. Like my journey across the state, the canal started in the shadow of Chicago and ended at the mighty Mississippi. Unfortunately, the canal was a financial disaster. I can relate to that.

The People's Palace
Joliet

In the 1950s, Liberace's clothes were as famous as his piano skills. He performed in ruffled tuxedos, frilled shirts and bejeweled capes that would make an emperor proud.

When he played at the Rialto, Liberace announced, "At last, a theater to match my wardrobe."

That's how they tell the story in Joliet, and when you visit the Rialto, you'll find it easy to believe.

Back in the days when movies were the nation's pastime, many theaters were elegant. But the Rialto was special. The entranceway was modeled on the Hall of Mirrors in Versailles, and the lobby was inspired by the Roman Colosseum.

"I've been all over the world. There's nothing like this in the United States," Constance Bailey, a Pittsburgh teacher, said as she walked through the lobby. After visiting the Rialto in the morning, Constance gave up an afternoon at the casino to return. She wasn't leaving without pictures.

"This is phenomenal, the gold, the marble, the chandelier. And the organ—you've got to hear the organ," she said.

When the Rialto was built, in 1926 (with air-conditioning), they called it a "Palace for the People," said Janie Lawson of the Heritage Corridor visitors bureau and a volunteer at the theater. Back then, Joliet was a railroad outpost. Now, as Chicago expands, Joliet is suburb. For those keeping score: Route 6, the Lincoln Highway and old Route 66 all meet in downtown Joliet. That's a magic moment for people fascinated by highways.

But for me, the magic moment was stepping into the Rialto. There are 18 marble-like columns in the lobby supporting a rounded ceiling and walls with scores of gold-inlaid figures. A grand chandelier, called The Duchess, hangs in the middle.

Then there's the theater itself, with frescoes in obscure areas so that every patron has something interesting to look at, and an original Barton Brothers organ. Enthusiasts and performers from around the world come to the annual Organ Extravaganza in April.

Comedian Red Skelton returned to the Rialto in his later years, just to see the theater one more time. He stood on stage and wept.

The theater, which was nearly torn down in the 1970s—was being restored when Skelton returned. He purchased the remaining 16 box seats and had them named for his family and friends.

In front of the theater there's a silhouette of the Marx Brothers, who tried, unsuccessfully, to raise chickens near Joliet before turning to show business.

Tour buses stop at the Rialto, and there are public tours, with an organ recital on Tuesdays. But the best way to see the theater is to attend one of the many stage shows here. They play the organ before every performance.

Instant Suburbs
Minooka

**W**est of Joliet, condos are sprouting faster than corn. Hundreds of homes are under construction and there are thousands more on the drawing boards.

You'll see developments called Mallard Point, Reflections and Indian Ridge on Ridge Road, near the tiny town of Minooka. Nearby is the giant Hunters West complex.

Amid all this growth, Mallard Point boasts of "country living." Maybe they're talking about the way it was before Mallard Point opened.

"None of that was here three or four years ago," said Harry Breen of Morris, which is just west of Minooka, where he grew up. "I knew everyone there. Now I don't know anybody."

Communities now charge developers construction fees to offset the cost of new roads, schools, sewers, police and fire protection that the new homes will need.

"There are 3,000 homes approved or proposed. That changes a lot of things," said Pat Graziano, editor of the *Morris Daily Herald.*

In Morris, folks watch the growth apprehensively. They know Morris could change, too.

"I've been here since '69," Bob Borgstrom said. "It's a nice, small town. I don't know where the keys to my house are. I haven't locked the door in years."

It's the kind of town that hosts an annual tractor festival, a corn festival and a dulcimer festival.

"The people here get behind every event there is," said Eric Davy, whose family moved to Morris when he was five.

"The people I grew up with—they all stayed here. And the ones that didn't stay come back a lot," Eric said.

Now they all wonder how much longer it will last.

If you're in Morris, stop at Romines R-Place. It's a very good truck-stop restaurant, and if you're lucky you'll see someone trying to put away an Ethel burger (four pounds with the fixins). If you finish it in an hour, it's free.

Construction near Morris

Wild Bill & The Preacher
Troy Grove and Princeton

For a while, Wild Bill Hickok and Owen Lovejoy lived about 25 miles apart in northern Illinois. I can't say they ever met, but it's possible, because the gunfighter and the preacher had something in common—their homes were both Underground Railroad stations.

Wild Bill, whose name was actually James Butler Hickok, was born in Homer (now Troy Grove) in 1837, the same year that Owen Lovejoy moved to Princeton, where he ministered to a congregation of about 200.

Young Hickok reportedly learned to shoot by protecting the farm from anti-abolitionist attacks. By the time he was 20, Hickok's wanderlust took him west, first as a stagecoach driver, then as a lawman, an Army scout and a gambler. He became a legendary gunfighter with an uncanny mix of speed and accuracy. His friends included sharpshooters Buffalo Bill Cody and Calamity Jane Canary. For a while he appeared in Cody's Wild West show, but he longed for the open spaces.

There are several stories about his nickname. Here's the one I like: In his early days out West, he was stuck with the name "Duckbill" because of his big lips. After a shootout, a woman called him Wild Bill and the name stuck—with some help from Hickok, who didn't particularly like being known as "Duckbill."

OK, that's actually a combination of two stories. But it is clear that Hickok was fond of improving his image, so both could well be true.

Wild Bill is buried in Deadwood, South Dakota, where he was shot

Wild Bill Hickok (public domain photo)

from behind in 1876 while playing poker. Yes, he really was holding aces and eights, now known as the dead-man's hand. Calamity Jane is buried beside him.

There's a monument to Hickok at Mechanic and Ottawa streets in Troy Grove.

The Lovejoy Homestead in Princeton is a different sort of memorial. The centerpiece is a quiet, graceful white house that looks as though it's never seen anything more dramatic than a family squabble.

Nothing could be farther from the truth, of course. Lovejoy was an outspoken abolitionist, and the house was a lightening rod for controversy. His prominence made the house one of the most visible stops for slaves traveling up the Mississippi valley to Canada.

Lovejoy was active in politics and was a founder of the Republican Party in Illinois. He knew Abraham Lincoln and was a special guest at the signing of the Emancipation Proclamation.

The Lovejoy Homestead is now a museum owned by the city of Princeton, which restored the building in 1970. The museum is on the north side of Route 6, just a few blocks east of Main Street, and is open weekend afternoons from spring to fall.

Here's one more thing Hickok and Lovejoy had in common: Hickok's father and Lovejoy's brother were both killed by anti-abolitionists.

Chuck Wagon Cowboys
Morris, Illinois

ut west, you're going to bump into cowboys every now and then. I met them in Colorado, Utah and Nevada. But I certainly didn't expect to find cowboys 40 miles from Chicago cooking beans at a chuck wagon. And for some reason, they didn't look out of place at a summer festival in downtown Morris.

Of course, Rusty Rankin is no ordinary cowpoke. Sure, he's from Texas. He wears boots and a bandanna and a 10-gallon hat. He's even got spurs lying around someplace.

But he doesn't have a horse, and he's never poked a cow in his life. It's the chuck wagon that fascinates Rusty. He was hooked the first time he saw one of these mobile kitchens in San Antonio, 10 years ago.

"I fell in love. I said, 'I will find me a chuck wagon,'" Rusty said when I met him at the festival in downtown Morris, which consists of a few blocks of shops near the Illinois River.

In San Antonio, Rusty ran a steel-fabricating business before he purchased his chuck wagon. He fixed it up and learned as much as he could about the cowboy life.

"I just wanted to tell people the history of the cowboys. We're starting to lose that history," Rusty said.

After he gave a few demonstrations in Texas, people asked Rusty to bring his act to other places. Now he travels across the country telling folks how cowboys lived back in the late 1800s.

"It's nothing like the movies. They weren't gunslingers and fistfighters. But that doesn't make good movies," Rusty said.

Most cowboys didn't even own a six gun—they couldn't afford one. Besides, revolvers were too heavy to lug around. When you're in a saddle for 12 to 16 hours a day, you don't wear anything you don't need. If a cowboy had a gun, it was a rifle.

And most cowboys didn't own a horse—they couldn't afford that either.

"Cowboys owned their saddle and their bedroll. And that's about all," Rusty said.

And cowboys were just about the least valuable things on the cattle drive. If they got on the wrong side of the trail boss, they'd be told to take their saddle and get out.

The horses were more important than the cowboys. The cows were more important. Even the cook was more important.

The cooks—the guys with bad tempers, bad teeth and bad breath—earned a lot more money than the cowboys, because food was important. If the food was bad, you had a lot of unhappy cowpokes on your hands.

Rusty talks about the cowboys with affection: "They were the salt of the earth, and their word was good."

Rusty travels with his father (Bud) and with Doc Lieber, who was once a movie stuntman. They do a few card tricks, sing some cowboy songs (singing helped cowhands stay awake in the saddle) and cook up some genuine cowboy grub.

"They drank boiled coffee. Not many people can make that anymore," he said.

The trio travels across the country, but Rusty likes small places like Morris.

"I do shows where 65,000 people walk by. This is better. The best part is having time to meet people," he said.

Or maybe the best part is being a 60-year-old cowboy.

Twister!
Utica

Dee Chase was outside watching the sky just before the tornado struck. It seemed safe enough. Twisters never hit Utica.

Then Dee's husband, Bob, saw shingles flying through the yard and rushed her into the house. They huddled in the kitchen for the most frightening 30 seconds of their lives.

"You could see this forever on television, but until you've been there yourself, you can't imagine what it's like," Bob said.

Dee recalls a rumble like a freight train and a howling wind that popped her ears.

"You could hear things hitting the house. I was praying," she said.

It was over as quickly as it began. But when Bob and Dee emerged from their house, they couldn't believe how much damage was done in a half minute.

Roofs collapsed, chimneys toppled, cars flipped over, trees landed on trucks and slammed into houses. The silo behind the Chases' house was carried across the Illinois & Michigan Canal.

Eight people died when the Milestone tavern collapsed.

"This is a small town. Everybody knows everyone who died there," Dee said. "It's such a shame; they went there because they thought it was the safest place."

After the storm, Bob and Dee walked down the street trying to help their neighbors. They weren't alone.

"Everybody was trying to help everyone they could," Dee said, adding that that's normal in a small town.

As Bob and Dee walked down the street, they saw how fickle a twister can be. One house was destroyed, the next untouched. Behind the Chases' house, a heavy container filled with oil and a light inflatable basketball hoop had been next to each other. The twister carried away the bucket and left the hoop.

All this in a town that hadn't seen a tornado in more than century. Twisters rarely touch down in the Illinois River valley.

Soon, aid workers arrived. First it was the Mennonites and the Amish, bringing their tools. Then volunteers from many faiths and organizations joined them.

"They were all so wonderful," Dee said.

When I arrived in June there was still plenty of damage from the April tornado, and eight crosses were part of a makeshift memorial where the Milestone once stood.

There were also signs that said "Utica's Back, Back Utica." People were working on their houses.

But long after the last building is repaired, Utica will remember the twister.

The Little Canal That Couldn't
Princeton to Moline

You've got to feel a little sorry for the poor Hennepin Canal. There are canals all across the nation, but none of them were more ambitious than the Hennepin, which was part of a grand plan to link the Great Lakes with the Gulf of Mexico.

It was a good idea, and if the canal had been built a little earlier it might have worked. Unfortunately, the Hennepin was doomed when it was completed in 1907.

Farmers had been lobbying for a canal to connect the Illinois and Mississippi Rivers since the early 1800s, but funding wasn't approved until after the Civil War and construction didn't begin until the 1890s.

It was just plain lousy timing. The world was changing rapidly while the Hennepin was under construction. As workers dug the trenches and built concrete locks on the Hennepin, other laborers were widening the locks on the Mississippi and Illinois rivers. When it was completed, the Hennepin was too narrow and shallow to handle modern barges. And by the early 1900s railroads were a fierce cargo competitor, taking heavier and heavier loads at lower and lower prices.

It was the perfect storm for the Hennepin, which was primarily used for recreational boats most of its life.

But some good things came from the Hennepin—very good things. Remember those too-small locks? They were the first American concrete locks without stone facing, an innovation later used in Panama Canal.

After the canal closed in 1951, the property was converted into what is now a 100-mile-long linear park with hiking and biking trails as well as historic and scenic spots. That's a very good thing, too.

I stopped at a lock right on Route 6. It was a nice, quiet, cool spot, but you'll learn more at the visitor center in Sheffield near both I-80 and Route 6.

From India With Love
Princeton

In India, Dev Vithalani and his wife, Hasumati, were doctors. Respected people in a small community. When they arrived in Joliet last year, Dev took a job at a gas station and Hasumati worked at a motel.

Why did they do it?

Because they love their daughter, Hetal.

When Hetal came to the U.S. to attend college, everyone—including Hetal—assumed she would return home. But she decided to stay here, so Dev and Hasumati packed their bags and joined her.

"India has a really family-oriented culture. They really feel bad when a child is alone," Hetal said. The family is together now, but it's not the same. Among other things, Hetal still misses the nightly dinners where as many as 60 family members showed up regularly.

"In India, maybe five generations live in one place," Dev said. "In our tradition, if you're old, the younger generation takes care of you. There are no nursing homes, just hospitals."

And in India, neighbors are like part of the family. If you don't like what's cooked at home, you're welcome next door, he said.

Dev and Hasumati worked separate shifts when they arrived in Joliet, where Hetal attends Lewis College. Last month, they purchased the Bird's Nest Motel in Princeton, a business that allows them to be together.

They bring a sense of their culture to the motel, which is just off I-80 on a commercial strip of North Main Street that runs from the Interstate to Route 6.

"When you are here, you are not a customer. You are our friend and our guest," Dev said.

Earlier this month, Dev's sister, Birju, and her two children joined them at the motel.

Davi, a 22-year-old with a crew cut and a broad smile, said he likes the U.S., especially the food. His younger sister, Poorja, says she'd return home in an instant if she could.

Her friends are in India and the food is better there, she said.

Birju would return, too. She misses going to temple and meeting with her friends.

And she misses the food.

Left—Dev Vithalani outside the Bird's Nest; Above—Dev at lunch with his family

Quad Cities Ice Cream
Quad Cities

 t's been harder than I thought to find farms that make their own ice cream, like the ones that dot New England. But the Quad Cities are an ice-cream oasis.

There are at least three outstanding emporiums here.

Whiteys may have the best ice cream in town, but Lagomarcino's is the local icon with hot fudge to die for and a humble custard stand called Country Style makes a mean malted shake. I stopped at all three, then I went back at Whitey's.

Whitey's has the best ice cream I've tasted since I left New England. I tried vanilla. I tried mint. I tried moose tracks with whole peanut-butter cups mixed in. I tried a shake. It was hard work, but somebody had to do it.

At Lagomarcino's, the hot fudge was as good as it gets. But don't ask how it's made.

Angelo Lagomarcino, the company's founder, bought the secret recipe from a traveling salesman in 1912 for what was then a big chunk of money. His wife was not pleased, to put it mildly. Today, Lagomarcino's is still a family-run business, and they still delight in telling that story.

They make the fudge in small batches and serve it in little pitchers along with the ice cream. It's nice to pour your own sauce, but it's really, really hard to get it underneath the whipped cream. I'll just have to try again the next time.

I heard about Lagomarcino's and Whitey's long before I reached Quad Cities. But Country Style was a big surprise. Charlotte Doehler-Morrison in the Q-C travel bureau told us we'd get the best malts we ever had there.

She was right.

Quad Cities folks are really lucky to have these three places at their fingertips, or actually, at their tonguetips.

Right, top to bottom—Lagamarcinos, Country Style & Whiteys

A kayaker in a Mississippi River lock

Mississippi Locks
Quad Cities

Walking into Davenport across the grated, iron deck of Government Bridge, I wondered how many others have crossed the mighty Mississippi here. I shouldn't have bothered with such thoughts—it's like trying to count the number of angels dancing on a pin. If you insist on doing the math, start with 18,000 cars a day on this 100-year-old bridge between Rock Island, Illinois, and Davenport, Iowa. Then add in pedestrians and trains and you'll get to hundreds of millions of vehicles and goodness knows how many people over the years.

Did I mention that this is where the first bridge crossed the Mississippi, which started a court battle involving a future U.S. president?

Railroads and steamship companies battled fiercely over the proposed bridge for years before it was built in 1856. Railroads needed the crossing, but steamships saw it as a navigation hazard, not to mention increased competition. The bridge was quickly enveloped in a court battle when a ship hit the support piers, knocking out one section of the span. The steamship companies sued to have the hazard removed. They hired a sharp lawyer who won case, but the decision was later reversed by the Supreme Court.

The lawyer was Abraham Lincoln, and the decision was reversed while he was president.

Today the bridge is part of an odd river crossing that begins with a causeway stretching from Rock Island to the front gate of the Arsenal Island military post. From there, you make a sharp left turn onto the bridge under the watchful eyes of sentries guarding the gate.

If you're adventurous, you can go straight ahead instead of turning left. Assuming you're not arrested by the sentries, this will take you to the military post, where you can visit the Arsenal Museum, with its collection of small arms and a history of the site. The island was a Confederate prison camp during the Civil War.

You can also head over to the Mississippi Locks visitors' center on the island, which has a terrace where you're almost close enough to touch the boats as they're lowered in the locks.

I was there on a rainy afternoon watching a kayaker make his way through the lock. He was paddling extremely hard—right behind him was a huge barge that wasn't waiting for him to get out of the way.

Tractors in all sizes at the John Deere Pavilion

John Deere
Quad Cities

Brian Thomas Moore at his magic shop

The Quad Cities—Moline and Rock Island in Illinois, Davenport and Bettendorf in Iowa— sit next to each other on the Mississippi like four neighbors rather than one big city.

For the most part, they're old river towns that mix their Midwest farming heritage with their river roots. You can go to the Mississippi Blues Festival in Davenport, or tour the John Deere Museum in downtown Moline or visit a Mississippi River lock in Rock Island.

I'm sure there are people who don't like Quad Cities. But I didn't meet any of them as I walked through the area.

Jim Hanks of Moline moved back to QC after spending several years working for John Deere in Atlanta.

"This is a good place for families; the pace of life is a little slower here," said Jim, who works as a guide in the John Deere Pavilion, a free display of farm equipment in Moline, where Deere invented the self-polishing plow blade that didn't get stuck in sticky Midwestern soil.

"The people are great. They're hard-working, friendly people—and you can drive across town in seven minutes."

Jim is an encyclopedia of Deere information. Among other things, he'll tell you that a four-row cotton harvester can reap 45 acres a day, replacing more than 300 field workers.

Some of these machines are truly gigantic. In the pavilion, kids (and adults) just love climbing up to the 15-foot-high cabs and sitting in the driver's seat. Of course, not many visitors have the $250,000 they'd need to take one home.

The big machines are fun, but Jim wishes people would spend more time at the exhibits about preserving water and land.

"It's what we have to contend with now," he said.

More than 1.5 million people have visited the pavilion since it opened in 1997, making it one of Illinois top tourist attractions.

There are also a John Deere collector's center, a John Deere store, a John Deere blacksmith shop and two Deere family mansions in the area.

All of them are open to the public.

On the other side of the river, magician Brian Thomas Moore returned home to Davenport after nearly a decade in Las Vegas. He loves Vegas, but his roots are here, Moore said.

"This area has grown, but it hasn't changed. If you actually get to know them, the people here are some of the friendliest you'll ever meet," he said.

Brian owns the shop where he bought his first trick. At the counter of Mr. Wong's House of Magic, Brian mesmerizes visitors with slight of hand and most of them walk out with a purchase and a smile.

But he won't sell a trick to someone who won't be able to do it. People who don't perform the tricks are the first to tell the secret, he said.

"There are two rules for magicians: never tell the secret and never do a trick twice," he said.

Not everything is wonderful in the Quad Cities. I met Robert Pillado walking along a nasty stretch of Kimberly Road in Davenport. We had the same thought: there should be sidewalks here. The Kimberly Road portion of Route 6 is a four-lane divided road with precious little room for pedestrians. Riding a bicycle here would be suicide.

"We're homeless. We've got to take the bus," Pillado said. The bus stops at K-Mart. If you want to go from there to Wal-Mart, you've got to walk on the road, Robert said. Wal-Mart has a sidewalk, but it's like an oasis in an asphalt desert.

This is a heavily developed stretch with shopping centers and big stores. Does no one have the foresight to see that some people might choose, or be required, to walk? Perhaps the folks in charge just don't care.

I've encountered this situation in several places across the country. The city's leaders, the developers and the merchants should be forced to walk in Robert's shoes—on the streets they built.

IOWA

Crossing The Big Muddy
Iowa

Y ou can see the country change after you cross the Mississippi. East of Casey, the land is a sea of cornfields dotted with stands of trees that look like islands in the distance.

On a Sunday morning, the road is quiet enough to hear birds chirping, bugs buzzing and cars humming on the interstate a mile away. Overnight, the corn changed from green sprouts to endless rows of golden yellow tassels. Blackbirds by the dozen sit atop the corn stalks.

The giant center-pivot watering systems are awesome to a city boy like me. These 10-to-15-foot-high pipes on wheels are like nothing I've ever seen. They stretch as far as the eye can see, spraying mists of white water from little wands hanging from the pipes.

I was severely tempted to jump under those pipes on the hottest day of the trek, which was in mid-July in mid-Iowa. Sweat poured off my face as I started walking west from Adair and there wasn't a tree in sight.

From Ohio to Illinois, folks told me that Iowa would be flat as a pancake and they were partly right. But on the western side of the state, Route 6 is more like a giant platter of popcorn—one little hill after another and they got worse as I approached Council Bluffs on the border. I probably should have figured that a place with bluffs in its name wouldn't be flat.

All That Jazz
Davenport

When you think of river music, cities like New Orleans, St. Louis and Memphis come to mind. Davenport, Iowa does not. But when showboats traveled up and down the Mississippi a century ago, musicians brought their new sounds as far north as St. Paul, Minnesota.

That's why Davenport is called Rhythm City and why it's the home of a fancy river music showcase, the River Music Experience, about a block from the Mississippi.

Hold that thought for a moment while taking this extremely short quiz.

Where was Jazz born?

A. In New Orleans bordellos, where piano players began mixing slower blues tunes with ragtime.

B. In funeral processions, where bands played festive songs on the way back from the cemetery. Behind the band, relatives clapped the beat and added improvised lyrics.

C. On showboats when musicians began slipping improvised solos into slow songs.

It's a trick question, of course. The answer could be all three, and more. The origins of jazz are far too complex for a simple definition. I learned that at the wondrous "Music Wall" in the River Music Experience.

You could spend all day at the 80-foot-long wall; tracing the music up and down the river with a click of a wand; listening to artists from the '30s to the 21st century; finding out what puts the jazz in jazz, the rag in ragtime, and the rock in rock and roll.

You can listen to dozens of singers, horn players and piano players at the Music Experience. Elvis is there, along with B. B. King, Fats Domino, Miles Davis, Roosevelt Sykes and W.C. Handy.

Julie Charkov of Des Moines took three teens here because they're all interested in music. When I met them, they were playing a bunch of hands-on instruments.

"This would be a great place to take a school group, we learned a lot about where the blues originated," she said.

But, for me, there was nothing like listening to Louis Armstrong, toward the end of his career in 1970, explaining why he continued to sing "What a Wonderful World" in a time of turmoil. Here's how he said it:

"Some of you young folks been saying to me, 'Hey Pops! What you mean, what a wonderful world? How about all the wars all over the places, you call them wonderful? And how about hunger and pollution? That ain't so wonderful either!' How about listening to Old Pops for a minute: Seems to me it ain't the world that's so bad, but what we're doing to it. And all I'm saying is: See what a wonderful world it would be if only we'd give it a chance."

You remember the song by George Weiss and Bob Thiele. It starts out:

"I see trees of green, red roses too;
I see them bloom for me and you
And I think to myself, what a wonderful world."

And it ends:

"I see friends shakin' hands, sayin' 'How do you do?'
They're really saying 'I love you.'
I hear babies cryin', I watch them grow
They'll learn much more than I'll ever know
And I think to myself, what a wonderful world.
Yes, I think to myself, what a wonderful world.
Oh yeah!"

That's a little of the flavor I'm trying to capture in our journey across America. Of course, Louis does it much better.

W. C. Clark at the Mississippi Blues Festival

Amana Colonies
Amana

 More than seventy years ago, Bruce Knowles was on a trip with his dad when he saw an endless row of men, each behind a horse, plowing a field near Homestead, Iowa.

"There must have been at least forty of them, side-by-side. They moved along the field together. One pass and the whole field was done. I thought it was remarkable," he said.

Bruce was just a kid, so his dad explained that they were driving through the Amana Colonies where people lived and worked as one family.

They didn't know it at the time, but Bruce and his dad were witnessing the last days of one of the world's longest-lasting communal societies.

The colonies were founded in the 1850s by the Community of True Inspiration—a religious group from Germany. Unlike the Bible-centered Amish, they believed in mystical contact with God. Families were assigned living quarters and jobs in fields, or in factories, or in the large community kitchens where everyone ate.

An Amana home

Bruce and his dad passed through the area just before the Inspirationalists voted to disband the communal life style in 1932.

"That was called The Great Change," said Mary Ann Fels, who grew up in Amana and remains an Inspirationalist. I chatted with her at a self service laundry in Amana, one of the seven Amana villages.

Mary Ann said the community changed on the exterior but remained a church-oriented group after the Great Change. Even today, men and women sit separately in the simple, unadorned Inspirationalist church. Until the 1970s the services were in German.

Amana (which means: to remain faithful) is still a small town, but Mary Ann said it turned into a tourist haven in the 1960s. The Amana Colonies (Amana, South Amana, Middle Amana, Homestead, West Amana and High Amana) are now one of Iowa's top attractions.

Stores line Amana's once-residential main street and there are craft shops throughout the communities. You can watch wool workers, basket makers and candle makers; but you can't buy a Big Mac. There are no chain stores in Amana.

Of course, if you have an Amana appliance at home, you already own a piece of the colonies' history.

Amana Refrigeration began here in 1934, partly because the colonists were skilled craftsmen who made fine wooden ice boxes. The company was owned by the Amana Society until the 1950s when it was sold. More recently, it was purchased by Maytag, which was founded in nearby Newtown, and Maytag was later purchased by Whirlpool.

There's a display of Amana products at General Store Appliances in Amana.

Lloy Hand at work

The Cornman of Des Moines
Des Moines, Iowa

 Every morning, when the corn is good and high, Lloy Hand climbs into his weather-beaten pickup—the one with a homemade tent over the cargo bed—and fills the truck with fresh corn. Then he heads to a Des Moines parking lot, where he sits on a plastic Valvoline can in the back of the truck and waits for customers.

Not bad for a 92-year-old guy missing a kneecap in his right leg and two fingers on his left hand.

But it's no big deal to Lloy. He's glad to be working again after the kneecap was removed in 1985.

"This is just something to do," said Lloy, who's been selling corn since he got back on his feet in 1992. Even now, he hobbles around on a crutch and has a stepladder to help him climb into the pickup. Each step on the ladder is precarious, but Lloy won't take a helping hand.

He says the knee still hurts, especially in humid weather. He'll roll up his overalls to show you the foot-long, jagged scar and the empty spot where there should be a kneecap.

Lloy still does things the old way. He records every sale in a ledger.

"See, I'm prepared for everything," he said as he grabbed a ruler hanging from the side of the tent to draw a new column in the ledger.

He sold 25 dozen the first day of the season in early July. Within a week he was up to 40 dozen.

"Today I bought 50 dozen. I've got three dozen left, and then I'm going home," he said. "Home" is in nearby Elkhart.

Lloy is an antique of sorts; a reminder of Des Moines before the outskirts became a sea of highways, malls and cookie-cutter stores.

"He's become quite a fixture," said Charlie Mathis of East Des Moines. Like Lloy, Charlie's been around long enough to remember Des Moines when it was a small city and downtown was the hub.

"This was the far edge of town when I first came here," Charlie said standing next to Lloy's truck on Euclid Ave. a mile or two from center city.

Of course that was 50 years ago. The city is battling to remain a hub despite suburban flight. There are now thirty-story skyscrapers downtown. There's a new civic center, a new sports arena and a new convention center. Tying it all together is an enclosed 3.5 mile skywalk that covers 30 blocks and connects dozens of buildings.

Lloy said Des Moines is growing out and the suburbs are growing in.

"It's just getting too damn big. There's places where the city limits meet," Lloy said. That will sound strange to anyone from the East, where every town bumps up against another. But there are plenty of unincorporated areas out here.

Now, here's Lloy's formula for a long life.

"Stay single! Keep out of the beer parlors and do not smoke," the lifelong bachelor said, pointing a finger at me as though he were Uncle Sam on an old recruiting poster.

And one other thing.

"Drink lots of milk. I drink about three gallons of whole milk a week."

P.H.A.T. Daddy's
Marengo

Every Thursday night at P.H.A.T. Daddy's restaurant, guitar and banjo players gather from near and far for a pick-up session. If you can play, come on in and set right down. Everybody's welcome.

This is music the way it's supposed to be. They play for enjoyment, not money. No one says, "We've been performing for 40 minutes, time for a break." They're having too much fun to take breaks.

John Johnson, a retired band member, travels nearly 100 miles to join in. "In a band, it's pretty disciplined. Here you just have a good time," he said.

The sessions started in a nearby real estate office, but soon they got too large. They moved to a tavern, then to P.H.A.T. Daddy's, where they ask no money and pay for their own beers.

Drop in on a Thursday and you'll see a bunch of guys or women dressed like farmers or doctors or salesmen or whatever else they were doing before they picked up their guitars and headed for P.H.A.T. Daddy's. About the only thing they have in common is the white socks under their loafers, cowboy boots or work shoes.

They squish together around a few beer-cluttered tables near the front door and play, mostly bluegrass.

They'll do standards like "Dueling Banjos" (a frequent request) and "Amazing Grace" and less-familiar songs like "Tonight the Bottle Let Me Down." Sometimes they'll forget the words when they try those oldies. That's part of the fun. In the audience, you're just sitting in on a jam session.

Cashier Debbie Jones works Thursdays just to be part of the moment.

"I love Thursday nights because they're here. We do get more customers because of them," she said.

Every week they play Debbie's special song, "Amanda."

"It always makes me cry," she said.

She wouldn't say why.

Jesse James
Adair

The hottest day on the journey came in mid-July in mid-Iowa. As I started walking at the Jesse James train robbery monument in Adair, sweat dripped off my forehead as though it were a leaky faucet. In the first 100 yards, the bandana I used to wipe my brow was so wet it was useless. And this was early in the morning.

The walk was mostly through cornfields—no trees. When I reached the town of Atlantic about 5 p.m. a temperature sign said 97, I was told it was 105 out in the corn fields. I thought: Is that all?"

And yes, there really is a train robbery monument. The plaque in Melvin Memorial Park says the 1873 heist was the first train robbery west of the Mississippi. Some folks claim it was the world's first robbery of a moving train.

Either way, it put tiny Adair on the map, and the town still celebrates the heist with an annual Jesse James festival. It's a big event with a parade, a chuck wagon dinner, contests and floats. They even name a Little Miss Adair and a Little Mister Gunfighter.

Here's the story of the robbery: James and his gang were already well known bank robbers when they heard that a huge gold shipment was heading through Adair on the Chicago, Rock Island and Pacific Railroad.

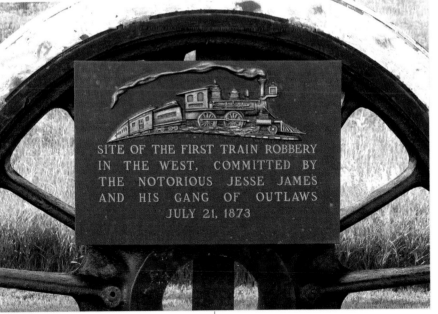

SITE OF THE FIRST TRAIN ROBBERY IN THE WEST, COMMITTED BY THE NOTORIOUS JESSE JAMES AND HIS GANG OF OUTLAWS JULY 21, 1873

On the day of the robbery they pulled spikes from rails at a curve near what is now old Route 6. As the train approached, they pulled the tracks apart with ropes and the engine crashed killing at least two trainmen.

Alas, our robbers didn't get the big payday they expected. The gold shipment had been delayed. James and his gang came away with about $3,000 collected from the train's store box and its passengers.

The robbery set off a furious hunt. A train-load of armed men soon arrived in Adair and the governor put a bounty on James' head. Eventually rewards offered by the state, the railroad and banks totaled more than $10,000.

Things didn't end very well for Jesse, who was shot in 1882 by one of his gang members who apparently thought collecting reward money was a better job than robbing trains.

The Adair memorial includes a locomotive wheel and a section of track that allegedly was at the spot where the robbery occurred.

The park is easy to find, it's at Exit 76 of I-80. Just look for the big smiley faced water tower. There's another Jesse James marker on Route 6 just south of I-80.

Above: Jesse James (public domain photo) **125**

White Poles
Dexter to Adair

More than a century ago farmers placed stakes in the ground to guide prairie wagons as they headed west through Iowa from Des Moines to Omaha, Nebraska.

Later, those stakes became white poles that guided cars along the roadway that eventually became Route 6, the nation's main coast-to-coast highway. Around here it was called the White Pole Road. Even airplanes used the poles as markers.

"Before they put these poles in, there was absolutely no way for anyone to know where they were going," said Jo Ellen Arn, retired newspaper reporter who is collecting White Pole Road stories. Back then—the road was little more than dusty or muddy path, she said.

That was a very, very long time ago, of course, and the original white poles are gone. But now white poles are making a comeback—this time as a marketing tool in towns like Dexter, Stuart, Menlo, Casey and Adair which are trying to lure drivers from nearby I-80 into their communities.

"We want people to stop off and see what we have. The white poles are a bridge between the towns," said Liz Gilman, a member of the White Pole Development Corporation, which was created to transform the idea into tangible results.

These are not glitzy, touristy towns, but Liz hopes people will come to see farms and fields up close, then stop for home-made pie at the Menlo Cafe or browse for antiques in Casey.

Liz and her husband, Ben, grew up in tiny Menlo where downtown is barely a block long. They remember when it was a bigger town with a grocery store and even a movie house. Like many young people, Liz and Ben moved away because there's little employment, but they commute here to work on the white pole project.

The development corporation's challenge is to get people who pull off the highway for gas or coffee to drive just a little deeper into the towns.

"If we can get just one percent of the people on I-80 to stop off, that would make a big difference," Liz said.

Youngsters painted the utility poles (as high as they could reach) white. A local resident created the signs to mark the White Pole Road.

Now the development corporation is promoting community events like last week's tractor run—where nearly 40 farmers drove their rigs along the White Pole Road. The farmers

One white pole

suggested the event and did most of the organizing.

"I thought it was a great idea. It creates activity," Liz said, adding that it "brought in people from 40 or 50 miles away."

There are about ten businesses in downtown Menlo. Casey isn't much bigger, but it does have a 40-foot-long, three-story high mural dedicated to the nation's 20th Century soldiers.

The mural includes nearly a dozen scenes. There's a large image of Omaha Beach on D-Day, a sunken battleship at Pearl Harbor and sailors laying wreaths. There are soldiers in a Vietnamese jungle, a Korean War soldier comforting a comrade, a Gulf War pilot, and soldiers raising the flag at Mount Suribachi, Iwo Jima. There's a WW I era image of Uncle Sam in a top hat and goatee and there's a WW II image of Rosie the Riveter.

In the center of the mural, giant letters say "Thank You, Veterans, For Freedom."

The mural is the work of area artist Ray Sorensen, a college student and it's worth a few minutes drive from I-80 to see it.

"You have a lot of people come by here to look at that," said Carole Moore who owns a nearby antique shop. When she's not in the shop, Carole, a Maine native, tends her ailing husband. It's not an easy life, but Carole has a smile, a laugh and a little advice for visitors.

"Life is too darn short. If you've got to choose between laughter and tears, choose laughter every time."

Scenes along the White Pole Highway

The Building Collector
Oakland

Some people collect buttons, others collect mugs or even cars. Penny Wright collects buildings.

Penny Wright outside her school house

Her backyard contains a small village: a restored one-room school house, a church, and the first public restroom in Oakland, Iowa. Off to the side sits her next project, an old wooden gasoline station that looks about ready to collapse.

Penny will spend months restoring that one too. Then there's an old jailhouse waiting to be moved to Penny's yard at the edge of a huge soybean field in Oakland.

"I just hate to see neat old buildings fall apart," said Penny, a professional house painter and interior handywoman.

Her passion for collecting began as a child when she and her mother made lists of the antiques they wanted. Well, they could never afford all of them, but Penny's house is overflowing with the little treasures she's gathered over the years, including dozens of red Scandinavian pots and pans that dominate her kitchen.

Penny's house, which also serves as a restaurant and bed-and-breakfast, is built around a century-old log cabin. After moving here, Penny wanted other old buildings.

"I said: 'I need a schoolhouse and a church,' " she said as we toured the buildings in her big country yard, which stretches for perhaps an acre or two.

Penny obtained the schoolhouse from a regional fair, which couldn't afford to renovate it. She expected to restore the building at her leisure, but soon a group of teachers called to book a luncheon at the restaurant—and a tour of the restored building.

"I said fine. Then I hung up and said to myself: I've got 30 days to fix this thing up."

It was a mammoth undertaking for one person. Penny sanded and varnished the floor. She restored the desks and walls and ceiling. She replaced the broken pot-belly stove and added kerosene lamps and an old-fashioned ceramic water cooler. It was worth it to see the joy in her guests faces.

"Some of the teachers cried when they saw it," she said.

Later, she spotted a dilapidated chapel six miles from her house.

"It was owned by two brothers. I just knocked on their door and asked for it." Two years later, they called and said: Come and take the building. The property was being sold and the land would be bulldozed within a few weeks.

The 1889 church was empty for 30 years.

"It was filthy; like an unclean barn," Penny said. "Birds were in and out. There was a dead raccoon. But I could see what it would look like when it was fixed up."

She restored the interior, replaced the pews, added electricity, and carved out a new bathroom.

"I had those pews in my garage for 10 years, in case I ever got my church," she said.

Now the church is a favorite spot for weddings. There have been 80 held there in the few years since the chapel was revived.

"We moved it here Aug. 19. We had our first wedding in September," she said.

Penny hasn't done much to restore the third building—an outhouse—which sits between the church and the school. It was once on Oakland's main street, and Penny thought it should be preserved as part of the town's history.

When she finishes with the gas station and the jail, Penny will probably begin looking for a general store or some other building.

That's what building collectors do.

Bottleman

Long before roadside cleanup projects were fashionable, Ernie Meyer was picking up bottles and cans along Route 6.

"It's a hobby," the retired Maytag employee said as he made his rounds in the small town of Victor, Iowa.

If you chat with Ernie, you'll find that his hobby is also a comment on life. He thinks Americans are no longer thrifty people.

"They shouldn't be throwing these things out," he said as he walked down the road to pick up a few bottles he spotted from his car.

"But that's the values of our country now. They say, 'What's the big deal about a nickel?'"

And that's just the tip of the iceberg, he said. Ernie sees a spend-happy nation that will collapse under the weight of its debts.

"We are going to wake up one day and the bottom will fall out. It's going to be just like 1929. I'm just sick about it."

Ernie picks up about 50 bottles a day. But he says his little effort doesn't change the big picture.

"We're over half-a-billion dollars in debt this year. We're all going down with the ship. But what can I do?"

Ernie had a triple-bypass heart operation in 2002. It's part of what makes him so outspoken.

"God let me live. I think I owe him something back."

Ernie was a prophet, of course. His fears were realized when the economy crashed four years later. And, yes, we have become a throwaway society. It's hard to recall that thrift was once a virtue.

To see how much things have changed, just check the roadside—before Ernie gets there.

Love Under A Bridge

Olivia's love story began in a Texas prison and, somehow, it grows stronger through her cold, hungry days and nights on the road.

She's slept in worse places than the concrete slabs under I-80 in Council Bluffs, Iowa, where I met her. Here, at least, the slabs are wide and dry.

The bridge was the latest stop on Jerry and Olivia's journey from the Deep South to Wyoming, then to Iowa. Most of the trip was on foot. Few drivers will pick up two people, their baggage—and their dog.

But Olivia would never abandon Champagne, the little brown mutt she rescued in Louisiana. She even made cloth booties to protect Champagne's paws from the hot highway.

It's been a harsh year, but Olivia doesn't regret marrying Jerry. Not for a second. They've grown closer while so many people with easier lives drifted apart.

"We're cold and hungry right now. Sometimes we've got blisters on the bottoms of our feet. But we're together and we're very, very happy people," said Olivia, a woman with rough skin but gentle, sensitive eyes. She huddled under a blanket with Champagne in her lap and a red bandanna tied around her forehead. A sweat jacket provided extra warmth and padding.

Nearby were Olivia and Jerry's possessions: a plastic cooler for food, two heavy blankets, a duffel bag, a backpack, and a few bags and boxes. The severed bottom of a plastic soda bottle served as Champagne's drinking bowl.

They met when Jerry was in prison. Olivia's son knew Jerry, so she wrote to him and later visited him.

Olivia is more than a decade older than 42-year-old Jerry (though she doesn't look it), and she was convinced their relationship would be over when he saw her.

But when Jerry was released, he showed up on Olivia's doorstep with roses in his hand.

"I was so nervous, I couldn't speak," she said. "Then I realized he wasn't looking at my age. He was looking at me. He has a lot of love in him," she said.

To Jerry, Olivia was a savior.

"My family stopped writing to me, but she believed in me. She has a big heart," he said.

I saw Olivia as I walked under the highway just east of the Missouri River. She waved. I waved. I climbed the steep embankment to a flat spot just a few feet under the thunder of truck tires on I-80 where it crosses over Route 6.

Jerry was on a nearby corner asking drivers for help. It was not a good morning. He was out there for hours but collected only four cinnamon rolls. For now, Jerry and Olivia would get by on canned food a passerby gave them the night before.

They could have steady food and a roof over their heads at a shelter, but usually they stay on the road.

"In the shelters, they try to keep us apart.

We don't want that," Jerry said with a hint of sadness.

It's been that way since they left Texas and Louisiana in search of a new life. Like his father, Jerry was a bricklayer and contractor. But the work dried up in Texas so they headed to Louisiana, where they had relatives.

When their truck broke down, they hitchhiked and walked. Jerry worked odd jobs as they made their way from Louisiana to Wyoming.

"Going to Wyoming was my dream. We wanted to build a house in the woods and be independent," Olivia said.

But there were few jobs in Wyoming, so they went back on the road.

"My dream is to get back to work," Jerry said.

When I met them, Olivia, Jerry and Champagne were on their way Providence, R.I., where Olivia worked many years ago at Brown University and in jewelry shops.

"It was so beautiful. I always said I wanted to go back there before I die," she said.

But she's not planning to die just yet. She believes they will get back on their feet one day.

"Of course it's going to happen," she said. "I say my prayers every morning. I know that as long as I do good things and don't hurt people, God will take care of me."

Iowa Hills
Atlantic to Council Bluffs

If anyone tells you Iowa's flat, tell them to ride (or, even better, walk) along Route 6 as it cuts through the state from east to west. They'll find a beautiful green countryside dotted with big cornfields, trees and, yes, hills.

I haven't seen this many hills on Route 6 since I left Pennsylvania. I suspect Iowans spread that myth about flat Iowa just to keep folks from moving here.

The hills got worse between Oakland and Council Bluffs. I didn't know it but I was walking through a geological oddity: Iowa's Loess Hills, one of the highest accumulations of loess soil in the world. There are a number of scenic outlooks in the hills, which stretch more than 150 miles along the Missouri river.

If you're wondering what the heck loess soil is, I can't help you. I looked it up. I still don't understand it. You'll just have to come here and see it for yourself.

132

Squirrel Cage
Council Bluffs

When you visit Council Bluffs, be careful how you talk to the city's black squirrels. They're the community's mascot and they're protected by law.

A 1875 ordinance makes it illegal to "annoy, worry, maim, injure or kill" a black squirrel.

And if you think it's a joke, just ask the guy who got arrested for annoying a squirrel.

Fortunately for him, he didn't wind up in the Squirrel Cage, Council Bluffs' strange jail.

The Squirrel Cage is a set of pie-shaped cells that rotate like a lazy Susan. The prisoners could leave only when their cells were lined up with the exit gate.

The idea was to give the guard more control, but the squirrel cage was never very popular here and a traditional county jail was built in 1969. The original contraption was the only three-story Squirrel Cage jail ever built. Naturally, it's a tourist attraction now.

Council Bluffs allegedly has more black squirrels than any other city—and now you know why.

The squirrel cage

Dancing Into History
Council Bluffs

he drum Orville Little Owl had been playing was silent. He sat, talking with friends between performances of Native American dances on a hot afternoon near the bank of the Missouri River.

"I do this, more or less, to bring awareness to people," he said. "We're still alive and we still practice our traditional ways."

A half hour earlier, young dancers hopped and pranced in the clearing while Little Owl sang and kept rhythm on the big drum.

It was a success, he said, because dozens of visitors learned something. They saw the grass dance, the fancy shirt dance and the jingle dance with a dress laden with metal that rings when the dress moves.

"People took part, they came up and asked questions," Little Owl said.

Little Owl was in Council Bluffs during the 200 anniversary of Lewis and Clark's expedition on the Missouri. They were literally dancing in the shadow of history not far from the spot where Lewis and Clark met with the Otoe and Missouri Indians.

The meeting, or council, along with the bluffs east of the Missouri gave the city its name. There's a monument honoring the meeting at Big Lake Park overlooking the river.

Some Native Americans see the expedition as a dark day, much the way Eastern Indians see Thanksgiving. The arrival of Lewis and Clark was the precursor to waves of pioneers and settlers that would nearly destroy the traditional life of Western Native Americans.

Today, they search for ways to live in American society while retaining their culture. For Little Owl, that means living in a square house instead of more traditional round one. It means finding what unites people and sharing what they have in common.

"We all pray to the same God," he said.

It means sharing the music and dance of his people. The dances have meaning, of course. The jingle dress, for example, is a healing ceremony.

"The traditional songs are like opera, they tell stories," Little Owl said.

Little Owl likes to meet people and talk about his traditions, but there's an undercurrent of sadness for what's been lost over the past two centuries.

"The Indian is the forgotten American," he said, adding that Native Americans are everywhere in our society, but we don't notice them or appreciate their importance.

"In white America, we are our brother's keeper."

He wouldn't explain that. He wants us to figure it out.

NEBRASKA

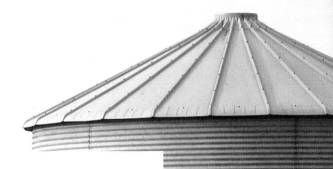

Please Don't Pet The Rattlesnakes
Nebraska

Route 6 is almost 400 miles long in Nebraska—that's nearly a month of walking beside cornfields that stretch 20 miles from one town to the next with no shade trees. There were days when I'd have given anything for a long drink of water.

I didn't know I was walking on top of the largest underground reservoir in the nation.

Nebraska sits above the mighty Ogallala Aquifer, a 175,000 square mile fresh water reservoir that stretches from South Dakota to Texas. The Ogallala makes the plains one of the most productive farmlands in the world, but unless we change our ways the aquifer will run dry in just a few generations.

There were a lot of other surprises in Nebraska including the remarkable capitol building in Lincoln and the huge ammunition depots in the middle of the state. And there's a wonderful museum triangle—the Prairie Museum in Hastings; the high-tech Arch spanning I-80, and Pioneer Village in Minden, a Noah's Ark of Americana.

Here's another surprise: Nebraska has a reputation for smelling bad, like the coworker who doesn't believe in deodorant. Actually it's the cattle trucks that smell bad—but there are a lot of them, especially in the middle of the state.

West of McCook, the road divides with Route 34 heading straight to Fort Morgan Colorado, while Route 6 makes a long arc before also reaching Fort Morgan. Route 6 is about 50 miles longer and I was tempted to go straight ahead. Luckily I stayed on 6, where I met some great people in the small towns of western Nebraska and eastern Colorado.

Not far from the Colorado border, there's a spot that local folks call the Little Grand Canyon. I won't debate whether it's really grand, but the best viewing spot is allegedly infested with rattlesnakes—there's even a sign that says watch out for the rattlers. Fortunately, I didn't see any snakes—nevertheless I stepped verrry carefully.

Five-Finger Salute

You can argue about whether the folks in the Midwest are really as friendly as they seem, but you've got to admit they'll wave to just about anybody.

Bikers, truck drivers, teens, little old ladies, farmers driving combines along the highway – they'll all wave as though you're their neighbor.

Traveling through Illinois, Iowa and Nebraska, I've seen them all. These folks have turned waving into an art form. The variations are endless.

There's the popular Lazy Finger wave: one finger lifted off the steering wheel.

There's the old-fashioned L-shaped arm with palm up, and there's the waving hand as though it were on a bobble doll. I even saw one driver offer a two-handed wave. Really.

There's the Cool Guy (it's always guys) who give you the pointing finger, the Gunslinger (pointing finger with raised thumb), and the Wagging Finger, like a schoolmarm chastising a student.

Motorcyclists offer an outstretched arm, in a "gimme five" gesture. That's my favorite, too. It takes less energy, and when you're waving all day, that's important.

This waving thing can become automatic. I absentmindedly waved at a mile marker once and a guy told me that his sister waved at a cow as they were driving by.

If they were in the Midwest, the cow probably waved back.

Gateway To The Midwest
Omaha

O maha was once the industrial giant of the Midwest, a place where beef and grain met the railroads. It was the second largest beef center in the world and not far behind in grain. The railroad connections earned it the name "Gateway to the Midwest."

Beef and grain aren't as dominant in Omaha today. The city is changing. It's becoming an arts and high tech center, but its blue collar roots are still strong—after all, the pro football team is called the Omaha Beef, not the Omaha Ballerinas.

The city's fortunes faded in the mid-1900s, but today you can barely move on the west side without seeing new construction and developments springing up. Downtown, there's a new riverfront park with a pond, paths and a boat launching area.

There are also plans for an elaborate footbridge across the Missouri River to Council Bluffs, Iowa. That's a very good idea, because I couldn't find a pedestrian crossing over the Missouri. I scooted across on I-480 (which is also Route 6) right beside many lanes of high-speed traffic. There was no walking area. It was one of the scariest stretches on the journey.

I don't know whether I was more afraid of being clipped by a truck, or having a patrol car pull up behind me with its lights flashing. About half way across I began jogging and by the time I reached the exit ramp I was in a full run.

On the way out of town I was surprised to find the road was hilly. That wasn't what I expected in Nebraska.

GAR Highway

ere's today's trivia question: What does GAR stand for? If you said the Golden Age of Reptiles, you made a courageous, but incredibly wrong, guess.

GAR stands for the Grand Army of the Republic. But unless you're really, really old you probably don't know that the Grand Army of the Republic was the support group created by Union veterans after the Civil War.

Now you're wondering why you should care. Well, once upon a time, the GAR was one of the most powerful organizations in the nation. It was the granddaddy of big veterans groups like the American Legion and VFW.

At its height, in the 1890s, there were 400,000 members—and they voted as a bloc. Until the early 20th century, the GAR was a kingmaker in the Republican Party. No one was nominated without its approval, and five GAR members went on to become president.

You can thank the GAR for soldiers' homes, the Department of Veterans' Affairs, and for a national holiday, Memorial Day.

And you can also thank the GAR for giving Route 6 a name as well as a number. Route 6 became The Grand Army of the Republic Highway after a lobbying campaign by the GAR and the Sons of Union Veterans of the Civil War, an offshoot of the original organization. In the 1930s, when they were doing this lobbying, Route 6 was a premier national road. Getting your name attached to it would have been like having your name on a sports arena today.

(Hmm. I wonder how long it will be before some company buys the naming rights to roads. The Taco Bell Freeway. The Joe's Pizza exit ramp on the Taco Bell Freeway.)

I encountered GAR Highway signs in most of the 14 states on my journey. There was even a GAR sign on a stretch of road in California that is no longer Route 6.

I also encountered real, live Sons of Union Veterans of the Civil War in several places on my trek. These soldiers march in formation, salute and call officers SIR! They take all this very seriously. They follow their orders, assemble and dismiss on command.

Sons of Union Veterans march in parades and they fight in battle reenactments. They talk of The War (no need to ask which one) as though it were yesterday. They seem so odd in a society that's moving at warp speed. But I think we need them, just as we need highways (and arenas) that remind us of who and what we are, not some products or corporations.

I met a dozen SUVCW members (there are 7,000 across the nation) on a hot summer day in Omaha. You could see the sweat on their wool uniforms as they gathered near a boat basin in a nice downtown park on the Missouri River.

"We experience what our ancestors went through to a small extent," said Commander Paul Hadley of Lincoln, Nebraska. "It makes you appreciate what they went through."

"It's a reminder that you're part of something greater than yourself," added Keith Rockefeller of Tecumseh. "When people see you in this uniform they ask questions—then we can tell our story."

And Route 6—the GAR Highway—is part of that story.

"It's a permanent, living memorial," said Dave Wells of Omaha, whose great grandfather fought for the Union. Dave is a historian for the Sons of Union Veterans, which keeps the Grand Army's memory alive.

Their story reminds us of a time when the nation was terribly divided. The factions couldn't settle the biggest moral question of the day and plunged into war. The war ended slavery, more or less. But a century later, there was still racial apartheid in the United States.

Maybe that's what all those GAR signs should bring to mind. Not that the North won, but that you can't always measure a war in those first days of victory. Sometimes the real work begins when the war is over.

The Sons of Union Veterans have put aside money for more signs, but states are wary of adding them. Still, you should be able to spot GAR signs, grand or small, all along Route 6. The most likely place to find them is near a state border.

Look for those signs. When you see one, tip your hat or nod your head a little bit. It's the least we can do to show that we appreciate the sacrifices those soldiers made so long ago.

Boys & Girls Town
Omaha

 ike so many kids, Enrique Mazone simply walked into Girls and Boys Town just west of Omaha looking for a place to stay. They took him in, of course. They always do.

Enrique flew in from Las Vegas because his mother wanted to get him away from the city's gangs. He remembers seeing the bright lights of Vegas as he took his first flight. Then he saw the darkness of the Midwest. He welcomed the change.

"I wanted to come here. My brother was here and he made it. When I showed up on the doorstep, they didn't know who I was," said Enrique, a clean cut teen with short, dark hair.

Here, they call these walk-ins "pilgrims." Sometimes they arrive with a note asking for help. Sometimes relatives call and say the child is on the way.

"We never turn any kid away. They may not end up here but they'll stay here until we find the best place for them," said Public Relations Director John Melingagio, adding that the Omaha center accepts only youngsters with desperate needs.

Walk around the campus and you'll never suspect this is a place for troubled kids. The 900-acre village includes a middle school, a high school, a post office, a fire department, a farm and more than 70 homes where the students live. It's one of 19 Girls and Boys Town sites across the nation.

Father Edward Flanagan, who founded Boys Town in 1917, designed the community structure before he died. He wasn't building an orphanage, he was creating a family. Old timers like me, remember the Boys Town movie starring Spencer Tracy as Flanagan and Mickey Rooney as a wayward kid. The village opened its doors to girls more than a decade ago and the name was changed to Boys & Girls Town. It is now known again as just Boys Town even though girls are included.

The campus feels like a prep school. You'll see students guiding visitors. Others are playing soccer on spacious fields. Some are at the farm feeding animals or cleaning stables. Girls are in the gym practicing volleyball and basketball.

"This is the best place I've been," said my guide, John, who wants to be a chef. "I spend a lot of time in the kitchen at our house."

Like John, most students live in a home with a married couple and half-dozen other students. Here they get love, understanding and strict discipline. There are rewards for good behavior and consequences for breaking the rules.

Many of the youngsters were abused, abandoned or neglected before they arrived.

"I've seen them coming from places where there was no hope to a place where there's hope," said Alex Franks, one of the surrogate parents.

Alex and his wife Melissa have been here eight years—long enough to have a houseful of young women return "home" for the holidays.

"The day a kid looks at you and knows you care—for a kid that has protected her emotions for so long—it's a wonderful feeling. Almost all of them turn that corner," he said, adding that the ones that don't make it can break your heart.

Father Flanagan believed there were no bad kids, only bad situations.

"Our young people are our greatest wealth. Give them a chance and they will give a good account of themselves. No boy wants to be bad," he told visitors.

Enrique is a good example. Today the six-foot-tall senior is quarterback on the football team, mayor of Girls and Boys Town and he holds an off-campus job.

Not bad for a kid who just showed up at the door.

A Rare Capitol
Lincoln

Folks in Lincoln will tell you that a panel of architects voted Nebraska's capitol one of the most beautiful buildings in the world.

At first glance, you might wonder whether the architects were looking at the right building. The 14-story capitol is an early skyscraper topped by a dome.

It's nice. It towers over the landscape. Still, it's no Taj Mahal

But look more closely and you'll get a different picture. Step inside, and you're surrounded by paintings and sculptures. This capitol is a museum as well as a working office building.

The artwork built into the floors, walls and ceilings tells the story of Nebraska from prehistoric to modern times. You'll find trilobites and mammoths etched into the floor of the rotunda hall.

In the vestibule, you'll see murals of homesteaders sitting by campfires, plowing fields and building houses—all in striking reds and yellows, the colors of Nebraska's sunsets.

The story continues with scores of murals and sculptures on the ceiling, floor, and walls of the foyer. You'll find memorials to people and events that shaped the state, like the schoolteacher who guided her students to safety during the killer blizzard of 1888. There's a state hall of fame where you'll find people like Father Flanagan, the founder of Boys Town.

There's more in the dome, where Norman Rockwell-like paintings depict the nobility of everyday people fighting poverty, healing the sick, and working for freedom.

Look at the outside of the building and you'll see history of Western

civilization told in sculpture.

The capitol tower rises above a flat two-story building that symbolizes the prairie. The lower building stretches for 437 feet, mirroring the state's 437-mile width.

If you tour the building, step out onto the walkway that circles the dome.

On a clear day you can see the entire city, including Fairview, the home of William Jennings Bryan, the soul of the Democratic Party 100 years ago. He was the party's nominee for president in 1896, 1900, and 1908. Bryan was a spellbinding orator and a populist who opposed big banks and railroads, earning him the nickname, The Great Commoner.

The capitol even reflects Nebraska's frugal heritage. It was built in the 1920s on a pay-as-you go basis. When the project ran out of money, construction stopped until the following year when new funds were appropriated. The building was paid for when construction ended in 1932.

But the capitol wasn't quite finished. The builders left room for much of the artwork that now adorns the structure. The homesteader scenes in the vestibule were done in the 1960s. The dome murals were completed in 1996. It makes you wonder what's next.

If you're in Lincoln, seek out a Valentino's Restaurant. Its trademark is a grand Italian buffet of soups, salads, pastas and all sorts of pizza. You will leave happy. I did.

Grain Elevators
Dorchester

Walking in the midsummer heat, you quickly learn to spot signs of the next town; the next water stop.

In the flat stretches of Nebraska I just looked for the grain elevators.

The towns along Route 6 grew up with the railroads. They're about 20 miles apart because that's how far a steam train could go before it needed more water. Farmers brought their produce to these water stops and the towns flourished. The centerpiece of it all was the grain elevator, which stored the farmer's crops and dispensed them to the trains.

Leave a town like Dorchester and you'll soon see Fairmont's elevator. It's a comforting site when you're alone on the road.

Unfortunately, those elevators are always a lot farther away than they look and it's a long time before you can see details on those silos. You know you're really getting close when you spot clumps of trees. The only time you see trees in this area is in a town or on a homestead.

Grain elevators are still landmarks, but their days are numbered. Small country grain elevators are disappearing; replaced by larger (and fewer) silos.

To a city boy, the elevators, like the center-pivot water lines, are an awesome sight. The elevators stand in the distance like sentinels, marking the location of a town. Out in the fields, center-pivots seem to extend as far as the eye can see. We're not in New England anymore, Toto.

A center pivot stretches into the horizon

Mighty Ogallala
Fleming

When you enter Nebraska you're above the mighty Ogallala Aquifer, a vast underground reservoir that stretches from South Dakota to Texas. They call the Midwest the Breadbasket of the World, but without the Ogallala the breadbasket would be half full—and that might be where we're heading.

Take a look around at all those center pivots spraying the corn and soybeans. The water is being pumped from the Ogallala. Without the underground water, this area would be marginal for farming.

In fact, that's what it was for most of the nation's history. Farmers began tapping the aquifer a century ago, but they didn't have the technology to draw the huge amounts we use today. During the arid dust bowl years, they just couldn't raise enough water to prevent massive crop failures.

By the 1950s, we had pumps, drills and irrigation systems to take as much water as we wanted from the Ogallala. And we did. Crop yields doubled and tripled.

It was a wonderful world for a while, because the Ogallala seemed limitless. But nature fills the aquifer drop by drop and we were taking out water gallon after gallon. By the 1970s experts knew the Ogallala was shrinking rapidly. Now, they say it could be dry by mid-century unless we change our ways.

Conservation programs and restrictions on farming have slowed the decline but the aquifer is still shrinking.

The Ogallala has been around for hundreds of thousands of years, in fact some of its water dates back to the ice age. Is it possible we'll use it up in a century? I hope we're smarter than that—I wouldn't want my great grandchildren saying we were the idiots who used up all the water.

As I walked through western Nebraska, I could see irrigation systems change. There were fewer areas being watered in the western end of the state and the systems were smaller and older. By the time I crossed into Colorado it was mostly dry farming, relying on what little rain nature provides. This area sits at the western edge of the Ogallala, where irrigation is strictly limited.

But somehow the folks here manage. It's odd: Farmers are people of steady, conservative habits. But they're in one of the riskiest businesses on earth. To survive these days, they need large spreads and machines that cost hundreds of thousands of dollars. New farmers start out in debt and can be wiped out by drought, flood, hailstorm, frost or infestation.

"I'd move out, but I owe everybody in town, so I can't," quipped Lowell Heath, who probably never, ever, thought of leaving Fleming, on the western edge of Nebraska.

His neighbor, Wanda West, wrote a poem about God taking a nap before finishing this part of the world. He awoke to find a hard-crusted, good-for-nothing patch of land.

Instead of undoing the mistake, God decided to create people who love this land the way it is.

"That's us," she said.

A side roller at sunset

Pioneers
Hastings to Kearney

Imagine you're pulling a handcart with all your possessions, including a child or two, across a 1,300-mile trail through the wilds of Nebraska, Wyoming and Utah.

There are hundreds of people like you on this trek—pioneers with no money for wagons and oxen. You're all heading west on a blistering summer day as part of a Mormon expedition in 1856.

Your leader, Edward Martin, gambled that the caravan could make it to Salt Lake before winter despite starting in late August. But your situation is getting desperate. You trade watches and keepsakes for food when you reach Fort Laramie, Wyoming. Even then, food is rationed when the journey continues. You worry about your children.

In early October, a bitter storm blows hail, sleet and snow as you cross the North Platte River in Wyoming. Thirteen people die in one night, many of them youngsters. You leave behind furniture, bedding, even blankets, to lighten the load as you desperately head west.

In late October, another storm forces you to a halt about five miles from the Sweetwater River where relief wagons are waiting. Yet another storm stops the expedition at the Devil's Gate rendezvous on the Sweetwater. It follows the survivors to Salt Lake. More than 100 people die on the journey.

The handcart caravan was ill-fated, but all pioneers faced hardships we can only imagine today. They forged across the Great Plains; they pushed and pulled their wagons over the Rockies—only to encounter deserts that were more dangerous than they looked.

There was no good time for the four-month-or-more journey. In spring, pioneers faced rain, mud and rivers too swollen to cross. In summer, they endured sandstorms, drought and baking heat. In fall, they risked early snow, like the handcart caravan. About one in 20 would die on the trip, most often under the wheels of a wagon or through illness.

Yet hundreds of thousands of men, women and children headed west between 1841 and 1869, when the transcontinental railroad was completed.

I encountered many reminders of these pioneers on my journey through Nebraska and eastern Colorado: museums, monuments and even deep ruts cut by hundreds of thousands of wagon wheels.

Just west of Hastings, you can almost taste the blood, sweat, tears and hopes of the pioneers at an obscure pull-off on Route 6. There's a faded sign marking one spot on the Oregon Trail, the most popular route west in the 1850s. Native Americans, trappers and missionaries blazed the trail. Later, settlers, soldiers, would-be gold miners and pony express riders all passed through here, most of them with dreams of a new life beyond the deserts and mountains.

They started in Independence and other points along the Missouri River and followed the Little Blue River into Nebraska, not far from Hastings, on their way to the Platte River. Other trails cut through Nebraska, but eventually they merged into the Great Platte River Road, a series of trails that paralleled the river.

"The rivers were their highways. There was always a source of water and you couldn't get lost," said Anna Mae Hagemeier, curator of the Overland Trail Museum in Sterling, Colorado.

The Old Pioneer greets visitors at the Archway

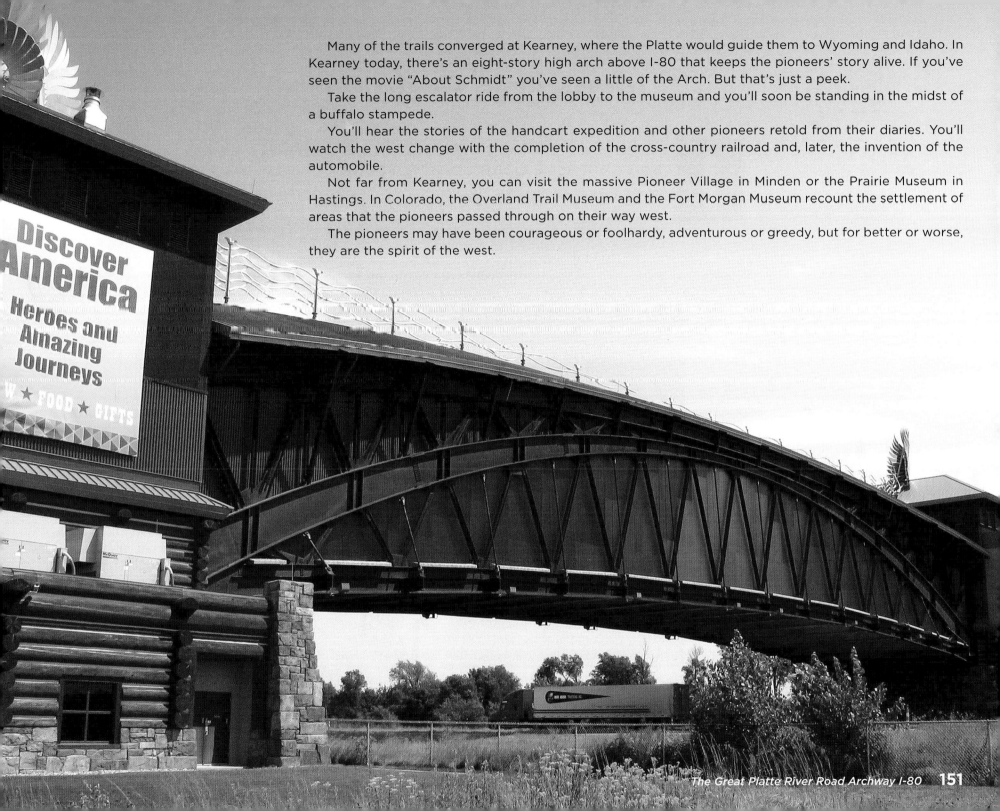

Many of the trails converged at Kearney, where the Platte would guide them to Wyoming and Idaho. In Kearney today, there's an eight-story high arch above I-80 that keeps the pioneers' story alive. If you've seen the movie "About Schmidt" you've seen a little of the Arch. But that's just a peek.

Take the long escalator ride from the lobby to the museum and you'll soon be standing in the midst of a buffalo stampede.

You'll hear the stories of the handcart expedition and other pioneers retold from their diaries. You'll watch the west change with the completion of the cross-country railroad and, later, the invention of the automobile.

Not far from Kearney, you can visit the massive Pioneer Village in Minden or the Prairie Museum in Hastings. In Colorado, the Overland Trail Museum and the Fort Morgan Museum recount the settlement of areas that the pioneers passed through on their way west.

The pioneers may have been courageous or foolhardy, adventurous or greedy, but for better or worse, they are the spirit of the west.

Incredible Essie

I'm not sure what people think they see when they spot Essie Garrett on the highway. She's 60, has dreadlocks down to her ankles, and she sleeps on the roadside at night.

I see a hero. What else would you call someone who devotes a good chunk of her life to helping other people?

I met Essie in McCook, Neb., while she was running from her home in Chicago to raise money for three Colorado charities. That's 1,000 miles, folks. About 35 miles a day for month. It made my little 20-miles-day walk seem like a morning stroll through an English tea garden.

Did I mention she was doing it on crutches? Essie injured her leg early in her journey. Most people would have quit, but Essie just hobbled along.

"There's a lot of pain, but I take comfort in knowing that what I'm doing is helping others," she said.

When she starts her day—at 3 a.m.—Essie focuses on the good things, like the war veterans who gave her the crutches and the wonder of the world before the sun rises.

"That's my favorite time. It's so still and peaceful," she said.

It's been 20 years since the former Denver teacher began doing 48-hour runs around the Colorado state capital to feed the homeless. Then she did longer runs, including Atlanta to Denver, Denver to San Francisco (and back), and Omaha to Denver.

"I try to do one a year," she said.

Essie Garrett

When we met, Essie was running for the Emily Griffith Opportunity School in Denver, the Sacred Heart House in Denver (for homeless for women and children), and the Kakapoma Milk Project.

Essie said many black and Hispanic women turn a deaf ear to AIDS information. She knows, because that's what she did until an organizer persuaded her to run for AIDS awareness several years ago.

"I'm hoping we raise enough money to have little areas where we can talk honestly. People have to be accountable," she said. She's trying to prod people to be involved in the world around them. That comes from her roots, growing up in a small Southern town where everyone pitched in.

"Today, I see us being about 'me.' I don't know how it happened or when it happened, but we've got our Starbucks and our cell phones and we're separating ourselves from each other."

Essie and her support driver, Clinton Classman (one of her former pupils), usually sleep on roadsides and eat on the run. A night in a hotel is a luxury.

Every so often on my journey, people pat me on the back and say, "Wow, you're terrific."

Naturally, I agree with them. But life has a way of putting us in our place. Essie is my place-setter.

Tall Tales or True?

In Hastings, Nebraska, Forrest Gump walked with me for nearly 20 miles. Well, his real name is Stan Mangers, but I'll always think of him as Forrest because he's full of stories. He talks a bit like Forrest, too.

"I have always wondered what life is about," he said with the hint of a drawl. "I don't wonder any more. I know there's an afterlife. I just live day-to-day and do the best I can. I try to smile at everyone I meet; you never know when you might change someone's life."

For Stan, life changed when he was in a car accident that claimed his girlfriend and left him seriously injured.

Keeping a vow to his departed girlfriend, he ran up to 10 miles a day for more than 130 days.

Later, he became involved with the Hispanic community and wound up driving a car to Mexico for a man he barely knew. They drove along narrow mountain roads and were stopped twice by the Federales. It was then that Stan feared the trip might be part of a drug scheme, but it turned out that his new friend was simply giving the cars to the people of a poor mountain village.

Stan became sick (drank the water) and was returning home by bus when police armed with automatic weapons awakened him at the border. It was Sept. 11, 2001, just after the World Trade Center attack.

Stan's bus was allowed into the country, but the border closed less than an hour later.

Stan has lots of stories, and they do sound incredible, but you never know: Life is like a box of chocolates.

Stan Mangers and Joe

Time Warp
Minden

hink of Harold Warp as a modern-day Noah, gathering the symbols of our world before they're gone forever. A bobby pin here, an airplane there; a ball point pen here, a refrigerator there—actually he gathered every major type of refrigerator and ice box made in the past century.

If you don't believe it, just visit Pioneer Village, Harold's incredible collection of just about everything that tells the story of American life from the mid-1800s to the late 1900s.

There are 30 buildings of trinkets, tools and treasures in this big time machine.

Do you like cars? You'll find everything from carriages to Corvettes here. The transportation building alone has more than 300 antique autos that give you an idea of the incredible amount of experimentation in the early days. You can find a steam-powered car, one with wooden wheels, and three-wheeled cars.

There are two more buildings of cars including more than 70 Fords and Chevys in the order of their development.

Want to trace the history of flight? You can find replicas and actual planes dating back to the earliest flying days, when planes were little more than bicycles with wings. You'll see early helicopters, ultra-lights and space gear.

And that's just a hint of what's in Warp's monument to Americana.

"We have a washing machine that was operated by a dog running on a treadmill—now that man really hated to do laundry," said Marshall Nelson, the village's general manager. Warp created a foundation to run the museum before he died a decade ago.

The museum includes the original Elm Creek fort (it's tiny, but it housed five families for two years). There's also a sod house from pioneer days, a pony express station, and a church. Warp bought many of these buildings when they were scheduled for destruction.

There's a carousel dating back to 1879. It's the oldest steam carousel in operation—and it still costs five cents a ride.

Visitor Berry Long was fascinated by the way everything at the museum seemed to fit into place.

"It shows how America was built," he said.

That's the way Warp wanted it. He wanted to show the evolution of technology. And Warp was part of that evolution. He made a fortune in plastics, rising from poverty in Minden. He invented flexi glass, Jiffy bags and Jiffy wrap. He claimed that he invented the plastics industry, and no one disputed him.

Most of the exhibits are in chronological order. You can see communication advances from the quill pen to the cell phone.

One building houses seven generations of typical living rooms, kitchens and bedrooms. Nearby, there's a hospital room with an iron lung, a scary old dentist's office, and an even scarier old beauty salon with those electric curling machines that look like torture devices.

There's old Doc Hapeman's office. Harold bought it when Hapeman retired in 1947 after more than 50 years as a country doctor in Minden. In the corner, you'll see Hapeman's house-call kit that included a horse whip, snow shovel and wire cutters (to get through fences).

Another building holds a huge collection of pens, toys and trinkets. There's a building dedicated to the evolution of ice boxes and refrigerators. And a section of another building dedicated to old washing machines.

Nelson said many people make return visits, bringing their children and later their grandchildren.

Jim Koop of Wallace, Nebraska, has been to Pioneer Village twice.

"It's and awesome place. My grandson points to things and asks me what they are," he said.

And he's old enough to answer the questions.

Nebraska's War
Holdrege, Nebraska

They say Nebraska is in the middle of nowhere. It's certainly the last place you'd expect to find German soldiers, Army convoys, ammunition bunkers & bombers flying overhead.

But "the middle of nowhere" was also in the middle of World War II. Huge troop trains rumbled through every day—and local women greeted the young soldiers with hugs and homemade food.

Thousands of bomber pilots trained in Nebraska airfields where corn had grown only a few weeks earlier. Many young farm women met beaus who later flew over France and Germany.

The nation made munitions in Nebraska and stored them nearby. You can still see the bunkers—thousands of them—dotting the fields around Hastings.

And Nebraska was home to more than 100,000 German prisoners of war. Many of them worked as farm hands in local fields.

"I think it was because we were out in the middle of nowhere. It would be hard for them to get very far without getting caught," said Sue Perry, who grew up in Holdrege, near one of the state's largest POW camps.

Due works at the Prairie Museum in Holdrege, which recently opened a wing that portrays life at the camp in nearby Atlanta. There were more than 200 buildings in the camp.

"I was shocked at how much land it covered," said Arden Walson of Atlanta. "It was a whole section of ground—that's 640 acres."

When the prisoners worked on the farms, many families took them in and fed them. Prisoners returned to camp with pies and homemade bread.

Back then, Maxine and Glen Hemelstrand owned a farm in nearby Gosper County, where there are plenty of families with German roots.

"We had four to six prisoners come to the farm in the winter. They were just boys, 16 or 17 years old," Maxine said.

A mural at the Prairie Museum in Holdrege

"From the very beginning, we invited them into the house. I guess we just thought it was the right thing to do. They were good workers and we wanted them to have a good meal, just like us."

She baked something for them to take back to the camp "probably every day. I made lots of cookies for them. They couldn't believe how well the Americans treated them."

Now, former prisoners return to Holdrege to see the camp site and perhaps meet some of the people who befriended them.

"This really is where enemies became friends," Sue Perry said. Not long ago, the widow of one former POW came to the museum in search of memories. She stopped cold when she saw a large picture at the entrance to the camp exhibit. She pointed to one of the prisoners in the picture and said "That's him!"

"She had tears in her eyes—and so did I," Sue said.

East of Holdrege, Hastings was the largest supplier of munitions to both coasts during the war. Military leaders wanted bombs and ammunition stored far from the vulnerable coastlines, and Hastings is just about midway.

Drive through the green-and-yellow corn and soybean fields along Route 6 and you'll see the grass-covered ammo bunkers to the south. You can't tell from the road, but they stretch back to the horizon. They're arranged in lines east to west, but not north to south so that any enemy planes coming from the north wouldn't have a straight row to bomb.

Not far from the bunkers, World War II pilots received their final training before heading to Europe. Overnight, farm fields were converted to airfields. Thousands of pilots trained at the bases; they moved out and more arrived.

To the north, military troop trains stopped at North Platte, where there was a canteen run by local women who prepared food in their kitchens and brought it to the trains.

"They say someone was there to greet every troop train that stopped," said Aloha Zimmer, who was one of the volunteers.

The women always had a few birthday cakes on hand for soldiers turning a year older.

"They appreciated that someone cared," Aloha said.

I asked her why we don't greet soldiers like that any more.

"It was a different time and a different feeling," she said.

Small Town Survivors
Lamar, Nebraska

 ooking at deserted Main Street, you wouldn't know that Lamar (population: 18) was once a bustling community.

"It was quite a little town once," Mayor Dennis Lenhart said as he sat on a metal folding chair in the community center, a former bank. Back then, Lamar had two grocery stores, a post office, a gas station and the bank. Route 6 travelers would stop for gas and farmers would come to town for supplies.

But the state moved Route 6. Now Lamar is two miles, on a dirt road, away from the highway and there are just a handful of farms left. The school has eight students.

There are a lot of towns like Lamar in western Nebraska and eastern Colorado. Communities here have been shrinking for more than a half-century.

Families moved out in the dust bowl years of the 1930s. Young men left during World War II and moved elsewhere after the war. Route 6 declined after the interstate was built.

The farmers who came to town for groceries and entertainment are gone. Small family farms have been consolidated into 2,000- and 3,000-acre spreads—and they're struggling.

"There used to be a farmstead on every quarter," said Dennis, who was wearing overalls and John Deere suspenders, "Now there are bigger farms with bigger equipment that takes less people."

The first farms were on quarter sections (160 acres). More than a century ago, the Homestead Act offered free quarters to anyone who lived on them for two years. Farming towns, each with their own grain elevator and railroad station, grew up overnight. The elevators, some of them 200 feet high with attached silos, still dominate the landscape, but many of the farms have disappeared.

"Everybody around here depends on agriculture in some way—everybody, not just the farmers," said Larry Wilson of Haxtun, Colorado, a town of 1,000 people that's managed to keep its population fairly even in recent years. Other communities, such as Holyoke and Fleming, Colorado, and Cambridge, Nebraska, and have leveled off after a decline.

The people who stay here (a lot of the young folks don't) love the quiet life and community of small towns where neighbors live next to each other for decades. One man told me that if you start a business in town, everyone will know it, and if the business flops, people will be talking about it 40 years later. He sounded like speaking from personal experience.

Nearly a century ago, Fleming (population 500) had two theaters, two hotels, four creameries, three grocery stores, and five filling stations. There were boxing matches in the theater and people traveled from all around for amateur hours on Saturdays.

Then came the dust. The 1930s drought and the constant winds covered everything with dust. Some farmers went to California, others went broke. Those who stayed, suffered.

"My mother would get up in the morning and wipe the dust off the table just so we'd have a place to eat," said Don Langdon, a Fleming native.

People hung wet blankets over their doors to keep the dust out, but nothing worked. Lowell Heath of Fleming came home from school one day to find his living room covered with two inches of dust.

"It was the one time I saw my mother cry," he said.

In Hamlet, Neb., the post office, the gas stations, and the one-room jailhouse are all gone. And most of the 50 remaining residents are old-timers.

"There's nothing to keep the kids here," said Clark McMinn, a Hamlet native.

But some people like the small communities. They enjoy the quiet and the safety. Some move here to escape cities and raise children.

"If you like to be more-or-less isolated, this is a good place," said Dennis, the mayor of Lamar, adding that the land is cheap.

"Some people come here from Denver or California; they think they they've stolen the house."

Lamar residents are divided. Some want to attract newcomers; others want to leave things alone. A few years ago, they started a fund to pave the road to town, but the road costs went up faster than their savings account.

Towns like Cambridge and Arapahoe, Nebraska. (both about 1,000 people) are courting newcomers.

"Tell them we have a lot to offer," a group of Arapaho residents told me. And they do. There are two modern homes for senior citizens and you can't beat their movie theater's ticket prices—$1.

The cross-country high-speed digital underground cable runs along this stretch of Route 6, and almost every library has a least a few Internet stations. Local investors are building a bowling alley and entertainment center in Cambridge, and an ethanol plant is moving into town.

Holyoke, Col., built its own theater and community center when the movie house closed.

"There was nothing for the kids to do," one resident said. The center includes a swimming pool, a basketball court and other activity areas. Local businesswoman Cherrie Brown said volunteers work at the theater to keep the prices down.

Over in Palisade, Neb., residents formed a credit union when the bank moved out of town. When their only restaurant closed, a group of local people bought it and started doing the cooking themselves. Now folks come from other towns for the nightly dinner specials.

These folks are here for life, but you have to wonder whether their children and grandchildren will stay.

Mayor Dennis Lenhart in downtown Lamar. **159**

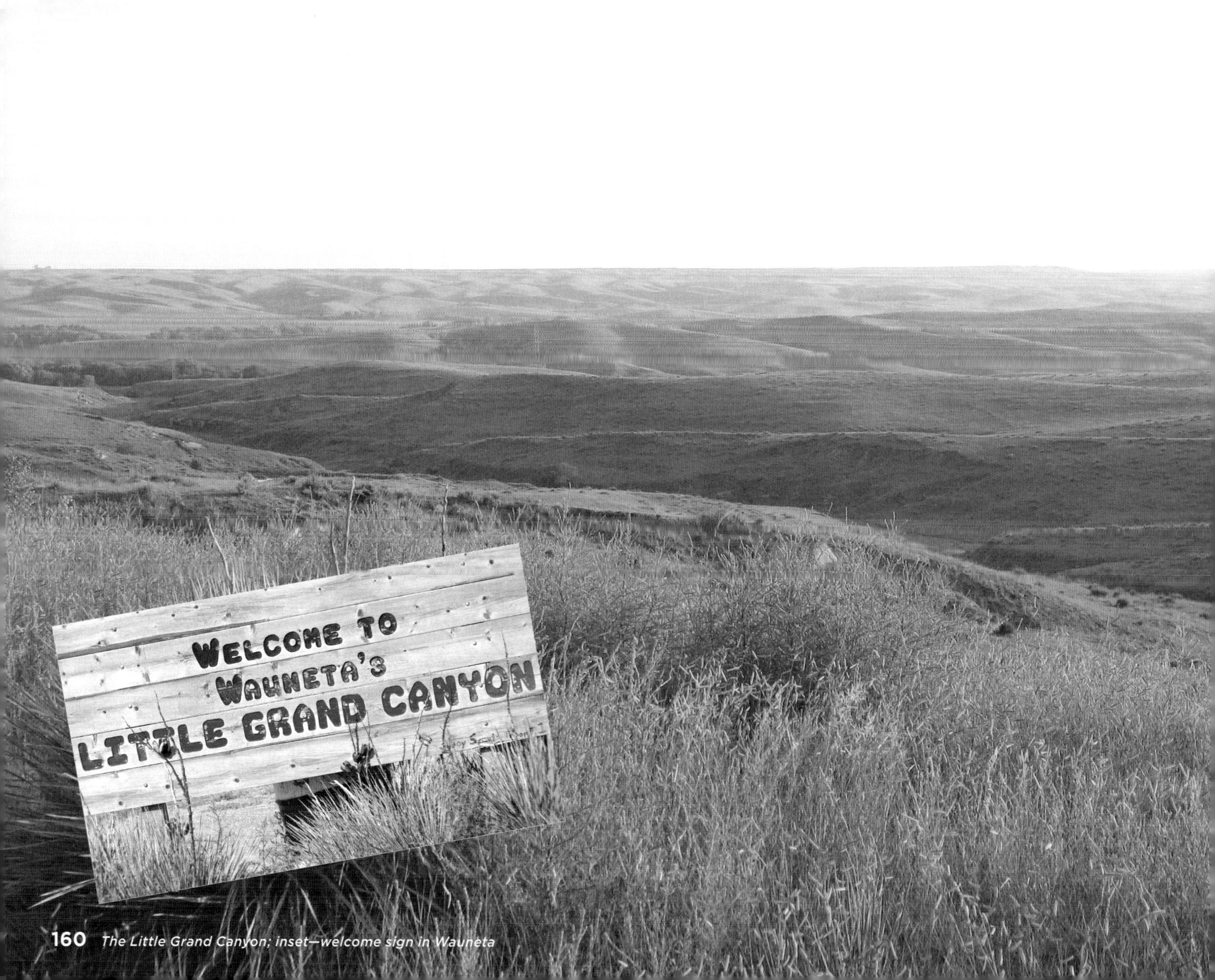

 The Little Grand Canyon; inset—welcome sign in Wauneta

Scary Cows
West of Lamar

They say cows are gentle creatures. But those folks never had a herd of the big beasts heading straight at them. Yes, cows can be scary.

Near the Little Grand Canyon in western Nebraska, I spotted a few dozen cattle pressing against a wire fence and bellowing. In the distance, three cowhands on horseback rode toward the cows and drove them behind a hill.

The show was over. I moved on.

A half mile down the road, I heard the cattle again, but this time they were much closer. The cowhands were herding them right down Route 6 to the Circle K Ranch.

There were 180 head of Angus, and they pretty much owned the road. Cars and trucks waited. Even the cowhands were wise enough to do their herding from the roadside. I scooted behind a guardrail as the creatures thundered past at a trot.

Wayne Krausnik of Circle K said they were getting ready to wean the calves from the adults.

At the ranch, two riders separated the cows from the calves and shunted them into different pens. It was the end of their lives together.

As I walked down the road, I could hear the cows bellowing a half-mile away. Was this just their way, or was it the cry of a mother losing her child?

Still, it was good to see an old-fashioned ranch instead of those giant feed lots that process up to 100,000 cattle. That's not a pretty sight—and it smells worse.

By the way, don't ask for a veggie burger in Nebraska. First off, they might not know what you mean. Second, this is beef country, ordering a veggie burger in Nebraska is like asking for a milkshake in a bar. It's just not done.

Trust me, I've tried it.

COLORADO

State of Mind & Mines
Colorado

You could say Colorado is the most beautiful state on Route 6—of course, thirteen other states would disagree.

I marveled at fields of sunflowers east of Denver, but they were outdone by aspens and wildflowers along the bike path through Vail Pass. And that was outdone by Glenwood Canyon along the Colorado River, perhaps the most captivating spot on Route 6. Then there's Rocky Mountain National Park about an hour north of 6. West of the mountains, snow melt provides water for the vineyards and peach orchards in towns like Palisade and Fruita. But beyond the snow melt, you're in the desert.

In the middle of the state, the Rockies are a regional gateway separating the plains of the Midwest from the deserts of the west. Denver has a touch of both regions with its cowboy image imposed on a city that looks and feels more like Lincoln and DesMoines than LA and San Francisco.

Colorado is also mining country, where silver and gold were once the currency of many small towns. Now the currency is white—snow white in the old mining towns that are now ski resorts.

Of course, the mountains aren't quite as beautiful when you have to walk over them. When I reached the top of 12,000 foot-high Loveland Pass (the highest point on Route 6) I figured it would be all down hill from there to California.

Boy was I in for a surprise.

Above Left—Watering spot north of Denver; Bottom Left—Lindzy Arnold, a tour guide at the Country Boy mine in Breckenridge

Skygrazers
Sterling

Sterling, about 80 miles north of Denver, was once a stop of the Overland Trail, which was 1860s version of a super highway. In those days, the trail was called the busiest road in America, carrying adventurers and pioneers thirsty for a fresh start after the Civil War.

Eventually some of these travelers settled in what is now Sterling, mostly as farmers at the western edge of the Great Plains.

Sterling is still a farming town, but there's more to it than meets the eye. Stroll through Columbine Park downtown and you'll spot five gold and brown giraffes growing out of a tree trunk. The 15-foot-tall sculpture is the work of Bradford Rhea, the area's best-known artist.

The tree sculpture, called Skygrazers, was Rhea's first big project. He carved the long necks and slender heads from the limbs of a dying elm. The trunk became the body and legs.

Some of the giraffes are looking up as though grazing in the sky.

It's easy to recognize Rhea's work. You'll find people, animals or spirits emerging from a central core, often in a fluid, circular motion.

"I try to achieve a spiraling flow to everything," said Rhea, who carved Skygrazers in 1984. It was so popular that Rhea cast it in bronze when the tree decayed.

"The community latched on to that piece," he said.

It was the beginning of a love affair between the artist and the city. You can find Rhea's works at the park, the library, the high school and the tourism center out by I-76.

Bradford Rhea at work.

Rhea moved to Sterling in the late 1970s with a different career in mind. He had a degree in nuclear medicine and was working at the local hospital as a laboratory technician.

"I quit my job, sold my car, got a bike and survived through people's generosity," he said.

Each of his works has a Biblical theme. The inspiration for Skygrazers was the verse, "Just beyond the clouds of doubt and chaos, they appeared, a congregation of spindling appendages fused in a mass of true belief with heads reaching in all directions."

In the library, Rhea's "Windlace" is a series of women emerging from a common center. The faces are progressively more detailed as they move up the sculpture.

"Here, I wanted to show the evolution of women," Rhea said.

Now Rhea is creating marble sculptures in his unpretentious studio in nearby Merino.

Kneeling on a scaffold eight feet above the floor, Rhea slowly chisels shapes out of the 10-foot-tall white rectangle of marble.

He thinks the piece will be called Transfiguration, but already, he's found faces in the marble that he didn't know would be there.

"When I dig into the material and I see something, maybe in a shadow, I follow it," he said.

"You make mistakes, but you keep chipping away and something comes of it—it's like life."

Sunflowers

From the crest of Wiggins Hill, 60 miles northeast of Denver, white puffy clouds were so low I felt as though I could reach up and touch them.

There's not much rain in northeast Colorado, but this area has its own dry beauty. Small sunflowers grow in clusters here, like bouquets scattered by the roadside. Sometimes they gather together in deep wide fields, like yellow and black armies of flowers.

In the distance, the Rockies are a series of mist covered gray peaks with white patches of snow spilling down the sides. Below the tree line, the mountains are dark, almost black. Stretching in front of these mountains is a sea of brown and gray prairie speckled with occasional trees and black dots of cattle.

The mountains must have been an awesome, and frightening, sight for the pioneers.

Denver

hen I first saw Denver, it was covered in a mist that spread out along the front range of the Rockies like the morning fog at an ocean town. Naively, I asked someone how often the fog sets in. Every day, was the answer. It was smog, not fog. Later, I walked into Denver through an industrial area on the east side of the city. This was not my idea of a Rocky Mountain High.

But downtown Denver is a different story. If you can't find a place to eat or something to enjoy downtown, you're not trying. There are hundreds of shops and restaurants on the 16th Street Mall, a car-free road in the heart of the city.

This was heaven to my wife, Pat, who wisely joined me in Denver. We walked up and down the tree-lined mall. We ate in bakeries, we window-shopped we bought trinkets, and we spent several hours in an old bookshop with big comfy chairs in Writer Square. When we were tired of walking we rode the free shuttle.

The mall is just a tiny slice of Denver. Along Colfax Avenue you'll get your fill of motels that have seen better days, pawn shops and quick-loan storefronts. It's not a bad street, but it's a very different Denver than the mall. Just off Colfax, I spotted a bustling arts area with cinemas, galleries and clubs.

But if you're on the road here, be careful. Denver drivers are fast and furious. Fortunately, their western-Midwestern hospitality returns when they leave their cars. On the way into the city one Denver man walked 10 miles with me, then bought me lunch and invited me to dinner. Another Denverite put me up for the night on very short notice when my hotel accommodations fell through.

Outside the city, folks were even friendlier. Merchants stopped to chat, drivers waved as they passed. It was like being back in the Midwest.

Maybe part of the Rocky Mountain High is Colorado's people.

Rocky Mountain Heights

Rocky Mountain National Park

When Lyn Thompson saw Rocky Mountain National Park 20 years ago, she knew immediately this was where she wanted to live.

"I knew I was home," Lyn said from her front porch overlooking the mountains in Estes Park at the eastern edge of the national park. Over the years she worked for the U. S. Park Service and the U.S. Forest Service just to stay in the big country.

"There's no other place I'd want to live. Anywhere I look, I can see mountains I've climbed," Lyn said as she sat in a big wooden chair outside the inn that she and a friend purchased earlier this year.

It's easy to see how Lyn fell in love with the Rockies. Driving through the national park is like having a front-row seat at Creation. You're surrounded by high mountains with rivers of late summer snow trickling down the crevasses. To the east, a series of sharp-edged peaks stand one after another, like giant ocean waves frozen in time.

Eons from now these giants may be gone. Perhaps they'll be reshaped by another ice age like the one that carved the Rockies 150,000 years ago. Later, rivers of ice came and went depositing rock and soil in the valley wetlands. On Trail Ridge Road you can see hills created by the debris.

They say that if you stand at the foot of Big Thompson Glacier you can hear the ice creak and pop as the glacier retreats. You can see streams of melt water flowing from the ice.

That's just one of the park's many faces. Drive, or hike, through the valleys and you'll see pastel green grass giving way to dark green aspens then to sheer rock dotted with white snow.

On a September evening, you'll see elk grazing in the meadows. Perhaps you'll spot a mountain lion or a bear where mammoths roamed 12,000 years ago.

But it always comes back to the mountains. Lyn has climbed many of the state's 14,000-foot-high mountains, but her favorite is Longs

Peak, which dominates the eastern side of the park.

"You reach the top and you can see most of the way to Kansas," Lyn said. "You can see most of the ranges and how they come together—it's what I had in mind when I came here."

When Lyn wants to catch a glorious sunrise she climbs the Twin Sisters, just north of Longs Peak. From the top, you can see the sun peek over the plains and watch as it catches the mountaintops creating a changing tapestry of light and shadow.

Of course, you have to climb in the darkness to reach the summit by daybreak. No problem for Lyn, who still looks trim and athletic at 40. She'll climb as long as her body holds up, she said.

People like Lyn think driving across Trail Ridge—a twisting 12,000-foot-high road—is fun. Can you imagine!

At the top of Trail Ridge, there's a stretch called the "the knife's edge" where there are drop-offs on both sides of the road. Park rangers have to remind drivers that cars actually do fit in the lanes across the knife's edge.

"A lot of people drive in the middle of the road," Lyn said.

I know how they feel. I don't like heights—and heights don't like me. I visited the park with my wife, Pat on a side trip from the walk. In a pathetic bid to prove my masculinity, I drove up Trail Ridge Road.

It was a pure bluff on my part, because a ranger had told me that snow (in the first week of September) had closed the higher parts of the road. So I drove up knowing I could manage the relatively short trip to Rainbow Curve.

At that very moment, they were reopening the road.

I drove and drove, thinking that the road would be closed around the next bend. We were no longer on the mountain side of the road.

Ski Country
Dillon-Vail

Downtown Frisco

Once upon a time, the little mountain towns west of Denver rose and fell with the booms and busts of mines and railroads. When the mines closed, the towns faded.

Some once-flourishing places are now just spots on a map. Silver Plume, where miners put together some of the best bands in the state, now has just a couple of stores.

Other communities—like Dillon, Breckenridge, Idaho Springs, Frisco and Georgetown—were revived by skiing and tourism. Today, their streets are lined with a modern gold: shops that capture tourists' hearts and credit cards.

Breckenridge has 2,000 full-time residents but surges to 45,000 in winter. Dillon and Frisco also grow from small towns to cities in ski season.

Some towns just happened to be in the right spot. Vail and Breckenridge sit at the base of huge ski areas. Idaho Springs is nestled close to several ski areas not far from Denver. Georgetown is the starting point of a scenic railroad.

Vail Village

On the ski slopes, you can tell the locals from the tourists pretty quickly. The locals are the ones with patches of duct tape. They can't afford to buy new ski clothes every time something gets ripped, said Lindsey Arnold, a 23-year-old Florida native, who's working as a mine tour guide in Breckenridge for the summer. She's part of an army of young people who come to the high country to ski, snowboard or hike. There's plenty of work for them during the season, but in October and April, everyone's out of a job.

The mountains are seductive, but it's not easy to live here full time, said Flo Raitano, former mayor of Dillon—which is 9,000 feet above sea level. There's snow 12 months a year.

"We watch Fourth of July fireworks in the snow. It takes a certain kind of person to live here. Most newcomers leave within five years, but those that stay love it," she said.

Flo and her husband (Ben, the acting mayor) have been here nearly 15 years. That makes them old-timers.

Of course, Dillon has always been a town on the move—literally. There are three villages under Lake Dillon's cool green waters—and they're all Dillon.

The town was founded in 1873, but moved twice in a decade: first to be next to the Denver & Rio Grande Railroad and later to be near the Denver, South Park and Pacific Railroad. The third move came when Denver created the lake as a reservoir in the 1960s.

Today, the lake is a tourist Mecca dotted with sailboats and surrounded by evergreen-covered hills. Beyond the hills, gray mountains loom in all directions.

You'll find hikers and bikers on the paths that circle the lake and connect the lakeside towns. In fact, the entire area is a web of bike paths, some of them through absolutely gorgeous mountainsides and valleys.

The path up Vail Pass travels through an alpine valley rich with flowers, aspen, canyon walls and rippling stream waters.

Now I know what Flo meant when she said the mountains are seductive.

The landscape changes quickly as you leave the Rockies. Heading west from Vail Pass, I emerged into Vail, a Disneyland of restaurants, shops, ski slopes and condominiums. From there, the mountains got smaller and in one quick turn they morphed into canyons, getting deeper and deeper until I reached glorious Glenwood Canyon.

173

The Colorado River and I-80 in Glenwood Canyon

Glenwood Canyon
Glenwood Springs

Hanging Lake in Glenwood Canyon

 've traveled across the United States, and nothing has beguiled me more than Glenwood Canyon. Not Cape Cod. Not the Appalachians, the Rockies, nor anything in between.

There may be more awesome canyons, but the bicycle/hiking path—and Interstate 70—through Glenwood is an incredible partnership of man and nature.

This stretch of highway opened decades after most of the Interstate system was completed. It was a long time coming because architects and engineers spent years designing ways to preserve the canyon—and they got it right. In some spots, the road hangs on the sheer canyon-side, like one of those kitchen tables that fold down from the wall.

The bike path sometimes runs alongside the highway and sometimes below it—but always next to the Colorado River. It was the closest I've ever come to recapturing the wonder of rafting down the Colorado through the Grand Canyon many decades ago. You feel it's a privilege just to be here, a place where the gods might have gathered eons ago.

If it weren't for the hum of I-70 traffic, this might have been better than rafting. On foot, you can take a long look at the high walls dotted with caves and jagged rocks.

In one spot, I saw columns jutting out like castle after castle in a row as far as I could see. Not far away, tiers of rocks formed an enormous stairway leading up the wall.

As I went deeper into the 12-mile canyon, I had to bend my neck to see the tree-covered top. At my feet there were piles of rock and rubble from slides.

It's hard to believe the sleepy Colorado has carved so deeply into the earth. The walls are made of hundreds of one-foot (or more) thick wafers of rock, each with its own geological story to tell. Sometimes the wafers are twisted sideways from some enormous event millions of years ago, a hint that the river wasn't the only thing creating the canyon.

Halfway through the canyon, you can climb to Hanging Lake, a pristine pond near the edge of a canyon wall. Far below, a dam creates another pond on the Colorado.

When the flood gates open at Shoshone Point, water from a 100-year-old power plant (the first on the Colorado) rumbles and hisses and splashes down a steep 150-foot slide and enters the river in a white, frothy roar.

On this day, kayaks, fishing boats and big rafts share the river below Shoshone.

On the other side of the river, Amtrak and freight trains roll by, just as they've been doing since the 1880s. The idea for the glass-domed sightseeing train was conceived here by a passenger who wanted to get a better look at the canyon. The California Zephyr began using the domed cars in the late 1940s.

If you're driving, you can pull off into several canyon rest stops. The best are probably Hanging Lake and Grizzly. But wherever you stop, do yourself a favor and walk a bit beyond the rest area to get a real feel for the canyon.

You can also rent bikes to tour the canyon. Some Glenwood Springs bike shops will ferry you to the eastern side of the canyon, where it's a downhill trip through the canyon back to Glenwood.

Unfortunately, there are occasionally rock slides in the canyon and once in a blue moon huge boulders tumble onto the highway and walking path. Nevertheless, I will return here one day. Some places are worth putting up with little inconveniences, like wondering if you're going to die.

If you're terrified that a slab will squish you, go very early in the morning (about 5 a.m.) before the rocks wake up.

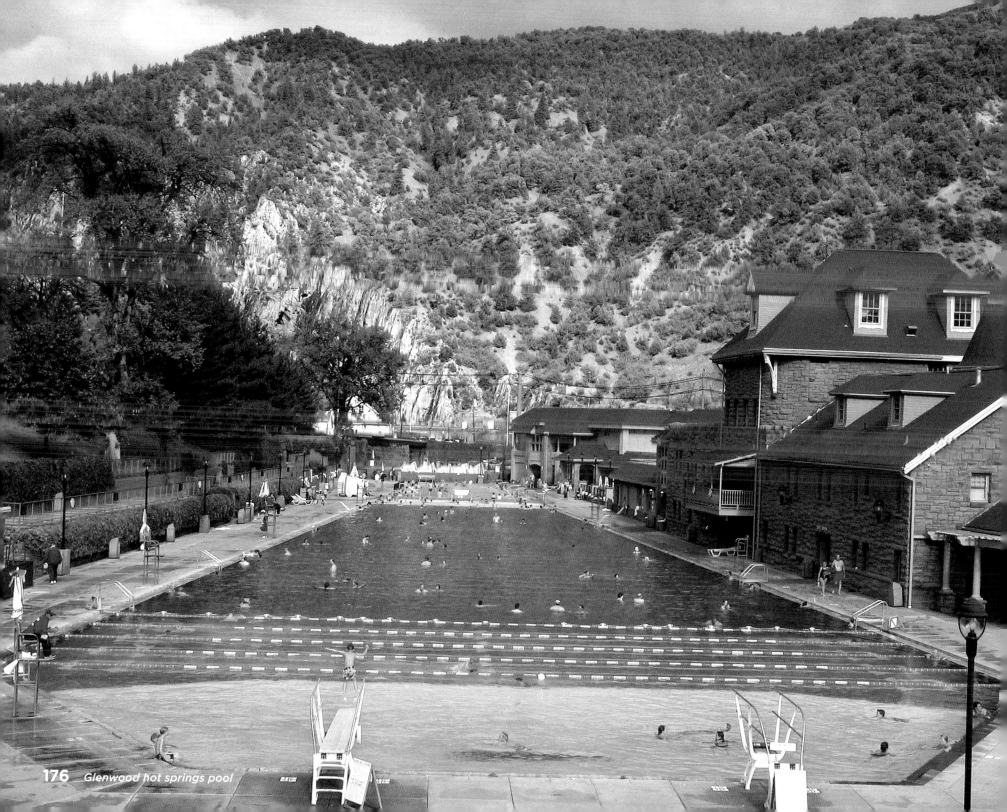

Glenwood hot springs pool

In Hot Water & Loving It
Glenwood Springs

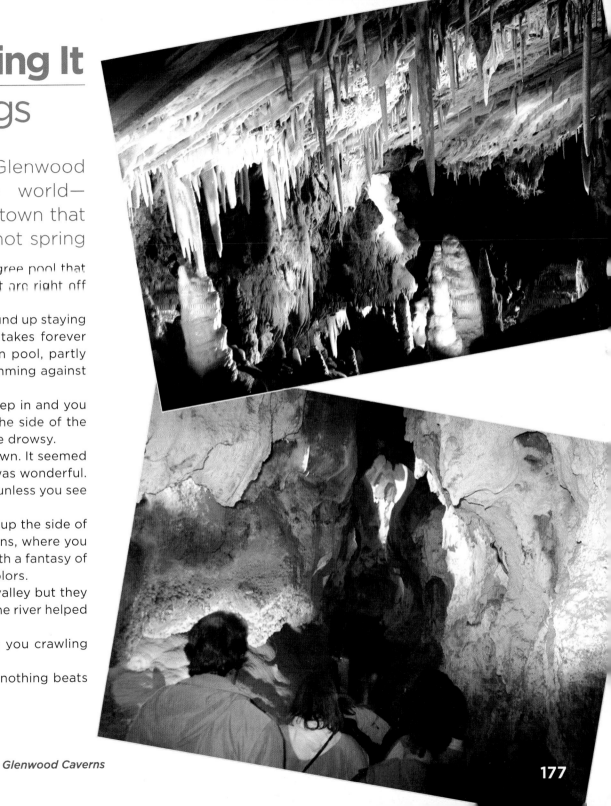

On the western side of the Glenwood Canyon you're in a new world—Glenwood Springs, a resort town that claims to have the longest hot spring pool in the world. You can soak all day in the 90-degree pool that sits between the old village and the new motels that are right off the interstate.

I intended to make a short stop at the pool but wound up staying for hours. It's intoxicating. And it really is huge. It takes forever to walk (or swim) from end to end of 135-yard main pool, partly because the sulfur-laden water is heavy. It's like swimming against the current.

There's a smaller pool with even warmer water. Step in and you may never want to leave. There are seats built into the side of the pool letting you just sit back and reeeeeelax till you're drowsy.

I was there on a cold, wet day with rain spitting down. It seemed like a bad time to be outside in a bathing suit, but it was wonderful. When you're in the pool the weather doesn't matter (unless you see lightning.)

At the western end of town, there's an aerial tram up the side of Iron Mountain that ferries visitors to Glenwood Caverns, where you can journey though narrow caves and a room filled with a fantasy of stalactites and stalagmites of all shapes, sizes, and colors.

The caverns are more than 2,000 feet above the valley but they were carved by the Colorado River ages ago, before the river helped create Glenwood Canyon.

For the adventuresome, there's a tour that takes you crawling through some of the smallest parts of the caves.

There are better known resorts in Colorado—but nothing beats the pools at Glenwood Springs

Glenwood Caverns

Abby's Auction
Eagle

More than a century ago, Doug Abbey's grandpa claimed 160 acres of dry land on the western slope of the Rockies. It wasn't worth much then, but the family turned it into a little empire.

"At one time we had 12,000 acres and 43 hundred head of cattle," Doug said as he prepared to auction the last pieces of that empire—the ranch house, the yard and everything his family accumulated over the years.

Doug and his wife, Betty, are moving to Mount Pleasant, Texas to be closer to Betty's aging mother. That was Doug's idea. He's sorry he didn't spend more time with his mother before she died.

This is the story of Doug and Betty and the end of their little empire.

There were all kinds of odds and ends in their sprawling back yard just west of Eagle, when I stopped by on a Saturday morning. There was the bus where Les Frimer stayed when he was down on his luck. Doug let him live on the land and Les—because he didn't take charity—gave Doug the bus.

"He stayed here several years. He died on this property," Betty said.

Behind the ranch house, visitors were inspecting bath tubs, chicken coops, farm machinery, a camper cap, a cement mixer, boxes and boxes of auto parts, more than a half-dozen vehicles, wooden fences, wood stoves, bicycles, a motorcycle, bedding, cabinets and scores of odds and ends that the family collected over the decades.

Betty said Doug did most of the collecting.

"I've been after him to get rid of this stuff for years. He's a pack rat," she said. But, now, she realizes that things like old license plates and vintage magazines are worth money.

"I've called this trash for years, maybe I'll have to change my idea of trash," she said.

Doug's ready to part with the goods, but the land is in his blood.

"What I'll miss the most is my willow trees and my irrigation ditch," he said.

That's not surprising. An irrigation ditch is a prized possession here.

"When you have land here, the water makes or breaks you," said Andrea Vesque, of nearby Brush, who came to the auction looking for antiques and bargains.

She had her eye on a glistening black and silver stove, but she guessed it would be out of her price range.

Andrea has known the Abbeys most of her life.

"My son-in-law's mother was raised on the ranch," she said. "It will be strange driving by and knowing they're not here."

Andrea and her daughter, Cathy, remember when Eagle was a much smaller and more isolated town. That was before I-70 was completed in 1992. The drive east was over the mountains. The drive west was through narrow, winding Glenwood Canyon.

In winter, both passages could be closed.

"We didn't have any hospitals. It used to seem like it took forever to go to Avon (the next town over)," Andrea said. Trips to Denver or Grand Junction were once-or-twice-a-year events.

Cathy left 15 years ago and she was shocked to see how much the town had grown when she returned. But it still has a small town atmosphere, she said.

"The one thing that hasn't changed is: this is still a great place to raise kids," Andrea said.

Doug Abbey recalls watching his kids, grandkids and great-grandkids playing in the irrigation ditch.

"I got—gosh I don't know how many—grand kids," he said. Then he began counting. "One, two, three, four, five. Eight! I got eight. And five great-grandkids and one great-great," he said.

He'll miss the animals, too. The dogs, the goats and the chickens. But he won't miss shoveling snow or tending the animals in winter, breaking open the ice so they can drink.

Most of all, he'll miss being on the land where he's lived for decades. Betty got a rare glimpse of that when she complained about moving everything out of their home for the auction.

"I told him the house feels so empty," she said. "But he said to me, 'How do you think I feel about my workshop?'" That's where he kept his most prized possessions.

At least there's a coffee shop near their new place in Texas. These days, Doug spends most mornings at the Eagle coffee shop with the guys.

"You know how that started? I tried to switch him to decaf, so he started going out for coffee," Betty said.

Doug isn't worried about how much money he gets from the auction. He's made millions selling off parcels of the family land over the years. Somehow, it hasn't gone to his head.

Doug and Betty: just regular folks moving on with their lives and saying goodbye to their empire.

Snowmelt
Parachute

Dark clouds were moving in from Utah; the worst one was just to my right as I walked along old Route 6 in western Colorado.

First came long, wispy cloud fingers reaching toward the ground. Then the clouds settled between two peaks atop the cliffs. The temperature plummeted, changing from early fall to mid-winter in minutes. Icy rain fell on my cheeks. Then one huge clap of thunder—with no flash—echoed through the notch.

When the rain eased, I looked back. The cloud was lighter now, and behind it, the two peaks had turned white with snow.

A few minutes later, the sky was clear.

All of this was in an area that gets just a few inches of rain a year.

"In two days there will be dust there," said Roy Savage, whose family owns a ranch near the town of Rifle. "From here on, it's a desert. Anything that's green, you can bet somebody's watering it."

Folks on the western slope of the Rockies rely on snow melt for their water. When the first settlers arrived, they cleared the mountains and hand-dug ditches from the snow pack to the valleys.

That was good enough for a century or more, but now the population is increasing and cities from Los Angeles to Denver are searching for more Rocky Mountain water. There just isn't enough to go around. Roy expects the competition for water to get worse in the coming years.

"We're probably into the 15th year of a decreasing snow pack," said Roy, who runs the ranch with his mother, Joan, and his brother, Dan.

The Savages have been selling off cattle in recent years because their grazing land doesn't produce as much feed. Dan and Joan say people who simply turn on a tap for water don't understand how scarce it is.

The Denver suburb of Lakewood requires homes to have green lawns—and the state won't allow homeowners to use treated wastewater for landscaping, Dan said.

"The state needs to keep up with the times," he said.

"They're just going to have to come to the realization that we don't have the water," Joan added. "When I came here, I had five gallons a day. I did the dishes, then I gave the kids a bath in the dishwater."

Dan and Roy remember those days—not very fondly, though.

Gas Bomb
Rifle

**N**early a half-century ago, the government exploded an atomic bomb inside a mountain overlooking the town of Parachute. The plan was to fracture a layer of hard-packed sand which trapped a reservoir of natural gas deep below the surface.

Well, things didn't work out as planned. The bomb went off and promptly melted the surrounding sand, creating a glass-like cocoon inside the mountain. No fracture. No gas.

The government, of course, told the neighbors not to worry. All the radiation was sealed inside the glass, like coffee in a thermos bottle.

Not surprisingly, people don't buy that story. They worry that undetected cracks might release contamination into the air or water.

Perhaps that's why folks in this area don't trust the government to protect them from the latest round of gas exploration on the western slope of the Rockies.

In the past decade, engineers found new ways to fracture the sand. They pump extremely high pressure liquids into deep drill holes to expand tiny cracks and release pockets of gas. The process is making the area a major gas producer.

"It's the Persian Gulf of natural gas," one resident said.

Wells are sprouting as fast as companies can find rigs to drill them. Almost anyplace you drill and fracture, you'll get gas. There's a problem, though. The pockets are small. To reach them you have to drill many holes.

At first, the Colorado Oil & Gas Conservation Commission limited drillers to one well for each 360 acres. Then, it was 160 acres, then 40. When there were proposals to reduce the area to 20 acres, residents recoiled.

Some joined a group called the Grand Valley Citizens Alliance, a local watchdog group.

"They estimate there will be 17,000 wells in Garfield County in the next 20 years. That will affect the environment," said Doug DeNio, an alliance member and former National Park Service engineer. He said residents worry about air pollution and water pollution from chemicals seeping through the fractures.

DeNio said few residents supported the alliance when it began, but the support has been increasing steadily, especially since the proposal to reduce the drilling area to 20 acres.

It was the local residents who convinced the companies that they could reach several pockets from one drilling platform by drilling at an angle under the ground, he said. This would, at least, reduce the number of wells. Now the companies claim it was their idea, DeNio said.

Few of the folks I talked with have confidence that the state is looking out for local interests.

"Everyone on that commission worked for or will work for an oil company in some way. They have too much vested interest," said Dan Savage, whose family owns a ranch near Rifle.

Savage can see both sides of the debate. Part of the ranch income is from gas wells on the property. But the wells also interfere with their traditional ranching business.

When the companies first started drilling, Dan's mother Joan actually stood in front of the bulldozers, he said.

And they're still fighting the companies. Not long ago, Joan sued the company charging it had shortchanged them on gas payments. She won. The company has to pay the royalties, but there was no penalty.

Dan said the state needs a more independent commission and more ability to monitor what the gas companies are doing.

But in at least one spot, there will be less chance to monitor. A gas company bought an entire canyon in Roan Cliffs, north of Parachute. It will drill wells and conduct its business behind a locked gate far from the nearest public road.

South of Parachute another company is planning to drill for gas on a mountain top—the one where they exploded that bomb a half-century ago.

A vineyard below the Book Cliffs

Grand Valley Peaches
Grand Junction

Millennia ago, the Colorado River helped carve a valley from the foot of the Rockies westward deep into the desert. In western Colorado it's called Grand Valley and part of the north wall is called the Book Cliffs because they supposedly look like an enormous row of books.

Travel along Route 6 and you'll be following the Book Cliffs for more than 100 miles from De Beque to Green River, Utah. Sometimes, if you catch the right spot in the right light, the cliffs really do look like a great big bookshelf.

Just west of De Beque, Palisade also got its name from the cliffs, but that's not what makes the area famous. Palisade and other nearby towns are the fruit basket of Colorado. You'll see orchards and vineyards all along the roadways. In summer, fruit stands as far away as Nebraska advertise Grand Valley peaches.

"There's really no place else in Colorado where you can grow fruits and grapes like they do here," said Kaibab Sauvage, 25, who manages a vineyard just down the road from the orchard where he grew up.

"The main thing is the weather. You need slow temperature fluctuations and that's what we have at this end of the valley," he said, as a breeze floated across the vineyard.

"This wind your feeling now comes along quite a bit and it keeps the air stirred up, reducing the risk of sudden freezes," he said.

One of his boyhood friends runs an orchard and ships peaches to Minnesota.

"The trick is to pick them ripe and still get them there fresh," Kaibab said. That means just a few days from the tree to plate. But the very best peaches are fresh off the tree in July and August.

I arrived too late for the peach season and most of the fruit stands were closed for the year. But Kaibab was still picking grapes at BookCliff Vineyard. They were the sweetest grapes I've ever tasted.

"We pick them by hand and put them into a cooler. The next morning they're on a truck to Boulder where the wine is made."

Wine making is a relatively new industry in Palisade, but it's growing fast. I saw at least a half-dozen vineyards along Route 6. Of course, they were outnumbered by the orchards and there were many more top-land groves on the mesa, just outside town.

Kaibab Sauvage at the vineyard

UTAH

Balanced Rock at Arches National Park

A Tortoise
Crosses the Desert

erhaps the strangest place I encountered on the walk was Arches National Park, which looks like it belongs in a science fiction movie. The arches, the balancing rocks, the strange colors and the quietness made me wonder if I had somehow wandered onto another planet.

Arches probably feels right at home in Utah, a state filled with out-of-place treasures such as petroglyphs, dinosaur bones and mirages. I like to think of Utah as giant time machine that transports us thousands of years into the past, when natives carved their stories in stone at Nine Mile Canyon and dozens of other spots. But that's modern history compared to the days when dinosaurs roamed a lush, nearly tropical land 100 million years ago. Today, you can find the big critters in museums and digs throughout Utah's Dinosaur Diamond.

The tropical land is now desert, which starts just about at the Colorado-Utah border, and continues, off and on, to California. It's easy to fall in love with the stark beauty; the vistas, and the solitude of these deserts. When it rains, withered plants blossom like a spirit rising, triumphant, from the grave.

Water is very important here, of course. But I didn't realize how important until I reached Price, where I got caught in downpour as I walked into town. I arrived, soaking wet for a get-together with some local folks and cursed the rain. Well, every jaw in the room dropped as though I had just sprouted horns. You don't curse rain in the desert.

In eastern Utah, old Route 6 follows the Book Cliffs west, then heads north at Green River for 100 miles to avoid the San Rafael Swell, an imposing plateau crisscrossed with jagged canyons. Some people call the swell a desolate spot, but it's as fascinating as Arches.

That detour around the swell meant a lot of extra walking, but without it I wouldn't have seen the dinosaurs at Price or heard how Butch Cassidy cheated death.

Near the Nevada border, Route 6 is part of what's called the loneliest road in the U.S. I don't know if that's true, but you can walk in the middle of the road because no one's just around the corner—when there is a corner.

185

First Desert
West of Mack, Colorado

Mack is the last Colorado town on I-70 before Utah, right at the edge of the desert. West of Mack, Old Route 6 is an abandoned road that runs parallel to the highway. Tiny pink and white cacti grow thorough cracks in the pavement. Mother Nature is reclaiming the road.

A few yards away, evergreens grow along the dry riverbeds. Beyond that, brown shrubs and brown grass blend into the brown earth. Just off the road there's a concrete obelisk that marks the state line. It was probably installed with great fanfare many years ago, but today it's as abandoned as the road, surrounded by brush, weeds and beer cans.

Past the border, there's a town that, like the unused sections of Route 6, seems to be headed back to nature. Buildings are abandoned, roofs and walls are collapsing. A one-time store or gas station is a hollow shell. In the back, junk cars and trucks abound. There's a rusted silo in the distance. No trespassing signs are everywhere.

One or two houses look as though someone might live there, but there are no people in sight. No barking dogs. No sounds.

I thought: This looks like the end of the earth.

Arches
Moab

Technically, Arches National Park is in eastern Utah, on Planet Earth. But I believe it's a misplaced chunk of Mars or Vulcan. How else would you explain this eerie collection of rocks and cliffs that look like they were created in a melting pot?

Arches has the highest concentration of natural stone arches in the world, but that's just part of the story. There are thousands of wonders, grand and small, in this 70,000 acre desert highland.

Just minutes after entering the park, you're standing in a vast pothole framed by a huge red sandstone wall called Park Avenue because its jutting edges look like New York skyscrapers.

Down the road, you'll find group of free-standing pillars where light and shadow work like an artist's brush. Look closely and you'll see the outlines of resting sheep seemingly chiseled in a nearby monolith. But that's not all. Giant rocks balance atop three pillars making them look like sentinels guarding the park. And we're just beginning our journey.

At Petrified Dunes, the earth is a brownish-red series of bumps for miles. It's as though you were a bug standing on the rim of a vast bowl of lumpy oatmeal.

It's hard to believe you're just a few miles from the Moab, a tourist Mecca where you can shop for clothes, crafts, Indian jewelry and, of course, rocks.

Back in the park, you'll stand in wonder at the base of Balanced Rock, a 3,500 ton boulder precariously standing atop a 70-foot high pedestal like an egg perched on your fingertip. It's

the most well known balancing act in the park, but it's not alone. There are scores, maybe hundreds, of balancing rocks here. Most of them are illusions.

They're not delicately balanced pairs of rocks, but single slabs where the base has worn away more quickly than the top. It's the same process that creates arches: soft stone wearing away before the hard stone above it.

From a distance, the Windows Arches don't look spectacular. But walk along the path until you're below South Window and look up. You'll see the sky framed in the world's biggest picture window. What a show!

Walk farther along a less-traveled path and you see the Twin Window- arches side by side, like a pair of cat's eyes.

For the hardy, the hike up to Delicate Arch—Utah's most photographed site—is worth the effort. Never mind that I climbed up as a thunderstorm was rolling in from the west. I had one eye on the trail and one on the clouds.

At the end of the 1.5 mile hike, there's a five-foot-wide ledge leading to the rear of the arch. It's not scary until you have to take the outside lane when you meet hikers coming the other way.

The wind was howling when I neared the top and it was nearly strong enough to knock me down as I reached the opening where Delicate Arch is a sky-high arc faming the valley below and the hills in the distance.

If you don't want to hike, there are two viewing spots near the road where you can see the arch from afar.

On my way down, people were still climbing despite the ever-closer clouds. It rained when I reached the parking lot and there were a few bolts of lightning in the distance.

I hope those folks made it down ok.

At Owl Rock, (which doesn't look anything like an owl) three young men were preparing to climb the 110-foot cliff.

"Moab is world-known for climbing. It's the sandstone that attracts us," said Kirk Hill of Ohio as he slipped into a harness before beginning his ascent.

Owl Rock is one of the most climbed surfaces in Arches. Kirk suspects the structure got its name because people like to climb it at night. For him climbing is about the thrill of accomplishment and overcoming fear.

"When you get to the point where it feels safe and you can concentrate on the challenge, that's when it's the best," he said. "It's like yoga, it just feels good."

Kirk eased into a fissure and wedged himself up inch by inch. As I watched from a distance, he disappeared into the crack and became part of the cliff. He was one with nature. That's the felling you get when you spend a day at Arches.

The park is more than Windows, Balanced Rock and Delicate Arch or the sites in guidebooks. It's looking out from a hilltop over miles and miles of canyon; it's the wind howling through the rocks, it's the hundreds of water-filled potholes on a plateau overlooking a wide valley, it's archlettes not big enough to be named, and It's finding your own figures and shapes in the rocks and cliffs.

It's meeting Mother Nature with her hair down.

Oasis
Green River

A couple of years ago, Dudley McIhenny of Salt Lake City bought some melons in Green River. They were so good that he couldn't resist stopping again when he was out this way on an archaeological dig this week.

That happens a lot in Green River. People pull off I-70 just for the melons.

"Everything here is just right for growing them," said Larry Bowerman, who was working at the Dunham melon stand on Route 6, at the eastern edge of town.

"We've got the river, the soil sweetens them up and they like the desert climate: cold nights and warm days." The whole town, in fact, owes its existence to the Green River, which starts in the mountains of Wyoming and travels through valleys, canyons and high desert before joining the Colorado River.

I tried some watermelon. It was very sweet. It was perfect.

Larry spends most of his day helping customers choose the right melon. The first thing he asks is when they plan to eat it.

"Is this a good one?" a woman asks showing him a cantaloupe. Larry looks at the orange hue and says yes. Then he feels it and changes his mind. "It's a little soft—that's the right color though."

He finds another the same shade of orange and the right texture, then he brushes it off and gives it to the woman. The cost: 30-cents a pound. Watermelons sell for 20-cents a pound.

He tells another customer that honeydews need to be "a little springy at the blossom end. Eat it right away if it feels at all soft."

Dunham is one of three big melon farms in Green River. They sell the melons as far north as Salt Lake and east into Colorado.

It was a busy day. A pick-up truck pulled into the driveway and three laborers unloaded a couple of hundred melons, tossing them, one-by-one, from the truck to a worker on the ground, then to the third worker who set them in the stand. When they were done, they headed back to the farm to pick more.

Green River once called itself the melon capitol of the world, but they don't do that here any more.

"Seems like every state has a place like this. A place on a river with the right soil and climate," Larry said.

I wonder if every state has someone as helpful as Larry.

Branden Wetherington weighs a melon at Green River

Pogue's War
Woodside

 ike a lot of folks around here, Roy Clay Pogue doesn't particularly care for the government, especially the U.S. Bureau of Land Management.

Roy is the last resident left in Woodside, Utah, which was once a railroad terminal and the largest town within 100 miles. He owns a ranch with 800 acres bordering the Price River. He also owns a now-closed gas station and a geyser that spouts water 40-feet into the air every hour or so. It was quite a tourist attraction until the state moved Route 6, taking it farther away from the geyser.

"We had a gift shop over there," he said, as we toured the property.

Not long ago, there was a herd of cattle on the ranch and that's how Roy's losing dispute with the BLM began. Roy said the BLM, which owns the land next to his ranch, told him to stop his cattle from wandering onto its land.

"They told me I had to fence off my land or get rid of my cattle. I couldn't afford 11 miles of fencing, so I auctioned off the cattle."

Later, the BLM began leasing its land to ranchers whose cattle strayed onto Roy's property, he said.

"When I complained, they told me I should fence off my property. They want it both ways," he said. Roy said a lawyer told him he could sue the BLM, but the government could tie up the case in court for years.

"I couldn't afford that, either," he said.

So now Roy has a few llamas, a couple of cows, a geyser and no fences to keep out the neighbors' cattle. Roy says 80 percent of Utah's land is publicly owned and people here don't have much say in how the land is used. It's a complaint I heard from a number of people west of the Rockies.

So now, instead of running a ranch, Roy survives mostly on his veteran's pension. Something's wrong with that.

Roy Clay Pogue, (right) his dad and their geyser

Real Dinosaurs
Price

 ere's what you need to know about velociraptors: they are ill-mannered creatures that should never, ever, be invited to tea parties because

they always come in packs. Not to mention that they are very likely to eat the other guests after stabbing them with giant hooked claws on their feet.

In "Jurassic Park," the heroes get chased by a group of these murderous dinosaurs. Real velociraptors were just as nasty as the movie version, but not exactly as scary—they were about the size of big turkeys. Director Steven Spielberg wanted something more threatening than turkeys, so he made his velociraptors twice as large. In Hollywood, you're allowed to create animals that never existed.

Well, shortly after the film came out in 1993, a scientist in Utah discovered the remains of a dinosaur similar to the velociraptor—except twice as big. Spielberg didn't invent a new critter. Nature beat him by about 100 million years.

It's not surprising that these bones were discovered in Utah, a dinosaur graveyard. Route 6 runs through part of Utah's "Dinosaur Diamond," an area filled with dino finds and museums. The College of Eastern Utah, alone, has uncovered nine previously unknown species during the last decade. That big velociraptor, by the way, is called a Utahraptor.

The nearby Cleveland-Lloyd Dinosaur Quarry has the richest concentration of Jurassic bones ever found. They've uncovered 12,000 so far, and they're still digging. Experts aren't sure why there are so many bones at Cleveland-Lloyd, but 250 million years ago, the area was a subtropical land with alligators, palm trees, vines and boa constrictors. Sort of like Florida with dinosaurs instead of condos.

Dinosaur man Reese Barrick

But that's no guarantee you'll find bones million of years later.

"You have to find dinosaurs living where there were sediments that came and buried their bones fairly rapidly—within one to 20 years," said Reese Barrick, curator of paleontology at the College of Eastern Utah Prehistoric Museum, in Price, Utah.

Barrick, who also teaches at the college, moved here to be closer to the dinosaur action.

"You get an opportunity to see real dinosaurs in an area where they lived. When you find something new, it really does excite you. You get a tingling," he said.

In the museum, you'll see bones or replicas of the newly uncovered species, including the Utahraptor and a massive unnamed brachiosaur whose neck alone was more than 15 feet long. You'll also get a peek at those nasty velociraptors.

You'll find prehistoric turtles with teeth, and dimetrodons (part mammal, part reptile) that lived before the dinosaurs. Kids can hunt for dino bones in a giant sandbox.

And you'll find that there are more questions than answers about dinosaurs. No one knows for sure what caused their rapid extinction. There are plenty of theories: climate changes, predators, giant asteroids, disease. It could be any or all of them.

Even the Cleveland-Lloyd quarry is a puzzle. Just how did all those bones get there?

Can you figure it out from these clues?

- Most of the bones come from the Jurassic period (roughly 130 million-150 million years ago).

Greetings from Afghanistan

I thought Nevada would be flat, like Las Vegas without the casinos. Instead it was filled with dry, rugged mountains, like Afghanistan without the Afghans.

You cross one range, walk through the valley, then cross the next range and the next valley. You do that a lot.

Crossing those valleys, I tried to figure where the pass would be in the next range. It's harder than it looks. From a distance you see a gap, but as you draw closer, it's gone and the road leads elsewhere. It must have been tough for the pioneers whose lives depended on finding the best place to cross.

The hills were a surprise, but I recognized the people—they were the same folks I met in the Midwest, just a little less outwardly religious

Several Western Shoshones from the Duckwater reservation stopped to offer me rides during a snowstorm. They were just about the only drivers on the road that day, and each of them stopped. The reservation's doctor shared his home with me. Good thing—I didn't have a place to stay and there were no hotels within 70 miles.

I walked on part of the Loneliest Road in western Utah and eastern Nevada, but Route 6 from Ely to Tonopah was just as lonely. I could count on one hand the number of houses I saw in that 160 mile stretch.

Ely

Once upon a time, Ely was the shining star of Nevada's mountain country. It still is, but the star isn't as bright.

Walk into the downtown Hotel Nevada or the Jailhouse Casino and you can play scores of slot machines for penny or a nickel. People sit there for hours and lose only a few bucks.

But there's a lot more than slots. If you want a taste of the old West you can eat in a cell at the Jailhouse restaurant. Or you can check out the stuffed snakes and other desert critters at the Nevada.

The six-story Nevada was the tallest building in the state when it opened in 1929. Now it's a symbol of Ely, a boom-or-bust mining town that was once a major stop for cross-country travelers.

Upstairs, above the casino, the corridors are lined with mining tools and you'll find the names of famous guests on the doors of the rooms where they stayed. Stephen King, Ingrid Bergman, Gary Cooper, Mickey Rooney, Tennessee Ernie Ford, Lyndon Johnson, John Schneider and gangster Pretty Boy Floyd all stayed here.

Wayne Newton's singing career started at the Nevada.

Jimmy Stewart's room was just two doors away from mine, so I peeked in. It was bigger and there were teddy bears on the bed. No Jimmy Stewart.

Before the interstate highway system, Route 6 and the Lincoln Highway, the two major east-west roads, met in Ely. Route 50, the old Lincoln Highway, still runs through the center of town.

"People would go through here on the Lincoln Highway, then head south on Route 6 to reach Los Angeles," said Evie Pinneo, executive director of the local Chamber of Commerce.

The influx of travelers, along with local gold, copper and lead mines, made Ely a bustling small city.

But now the interstates are more than 100 miles from Ely. When Kennecott closed its copper mines in the 1970s, the boom was over.

People in central Nevada live and die with the mines. Travel though the valleys and mountains here and you'll find the remnants of towns that disappeared when the mines closed.

"Today a lot of these old ghost towns are just sites. People go out and expect an old town like a Hollywood set. They find maybe an old shed. There are no barrooms with swinging doors," said Don Hickman, a history buff who lives in Ely.

Some of the towns burned down, others were dismantled when miners moved on to the next boomtown.

"Wood was scarce back then. When people left, they took the wood with them," said Hickman, who claims he was once the youngest dealer in the largest casino in Las Vegas, about 250 miles south.

After holding a number of casino jobs in Vegas, Don longed for a quieter life and opened an Ely car rental service with his brother, Jim.

Ely, with 4,000 people, is bigger than most of the boomtowns, so it survives the busts. Now the price of copper is up again and a Canadian company is opening a mine that will bring 300 new jobs to town.

Cheryl Geary, whose husband, Chuck, is the mine manager, said she's already getting used to the relaxed lifestyle in Ely.

"People here will speak to you in the supermarket. They may not know you, but they'll tell you about things like the doctors and the dentists," she said.

It's called Western hospitality.

Snow on Ward Mountain

Mining Town, USA
Tonopah

Jim Butler wasn't the most industrious guy in the world. He was a lawyer, but he didn't care for the long hours, so a century ago he set out to make a fortune prospecting in the hills of Nevada.

Around Tonopah, they say that one of Jim's mules broke away and Jim picked up a rock to throw at it. It was so heavy that Jim decided to keep it. Later an assayer said the rock was loaded with gold and silver.

Jim claimed most of the land in the area, but he didn't want to do the heavy work, so he let others mine the sites and he shared in their profits. Eventually, he sold his rights to a mining company and was a wealthy man.

That was the start of Tonopah, which calls itself Mining Town, USA. In the early days, it was quite the place. By 1916, there were 7,000 residents, five newspapers, 50 saloons, a five-story grand hotel, and 500 miles of mine tunnels. Wyatt and Virgil Earp moved here after the OK Corral gunfight, and boxer Jack Dempsey was a bouncer in Tonopah.

No place is closer to its mines than Tonopah. If you walk along Main Street or enter most any downtown building, you're probably standing atop a tunnel or shaft. A few years ago, a street caved in when a tunnel's shoring gave way.

Today, Tonopah is struggling. On the northern edge of town you'll find several closed motels. They catered to government workers when the Air Force base was booming. Now, even the grand Hotel Mitzpah downtown is closed.

To make things worse, owners rarely tear down an unused building. If they do, the property legally goes back to the mine owners.

"One thing that would help this town is zoning," said Al O'Donnell of the Chamber of Commerce.

The town's main attraction is a mining park, where some of the most important mines operated just a stone's throw from Main Street. More than $1 billion (in today's money) worth of material was taken from those mines.

In the park, you can peer down mine shafts and explore the buildings where giant pulleys were used to raise and lower men and equipment in the shafts.

You can walk above a long, deep trench where miners extracted silver close to the surface. Standing on a metal grate walkway you can look down at the timbers braced between the walls to keep them from collapsing. The trench goes deeper and deeper until it disappears in the darkness.

Tonopah is on a main road about midway between Reno and Las Vegas, so there's plenty of traffic. Local businesses just wish more people would stop for a while. Some of the modern hotels, the Hi-Desert Inn and Ramada, do quite well. But Al said he'd like to see more people visit the shops on Main Street.

If you're on the road here, why not grab a bite to eat and stretch your legs in Mining Town, USA.

CALIFORNIA

Promised Land
California

People say America is a big melting pot, but I think of California as a tossed salad where the ingredients keep their own flavor. Travel along old Route 6 from the Sierras to Long Beach and you'll see how these different worlds live side by side.

I entered the Golden State in mountains and desert, where it's not unusual to spot coyotes. A wolf crossed my path on the Sierra Highway. No one believes me, but it's true. I'm just happy the wolf wasn't hungry.

In winter, southeastern California is a cold, windy area dotted with small towns and friendly people who think going to Los Angeles is punishment. They like their country life. But the region is growing more than some folks would like. Old timers told me Agua Dulce's once-sweet water isn't the same because so many people are tapping the aquifer.

When I reached Mojave, the desert was behind me and LA's suburbs lay ahead. In nearby Lancaster, I saw commuters getting off trains in the center of town. Just 20 years ago, Lancaster and Palmdale had a combined population of about 40,000 . Today, the two cities total nearly 250,000.

From San Fernando south, the landscape is concrete and asphalt all the way to the ocean. Up north, people warned me to avoid San Fernando. Too much crime there, they said. Here's what I found on a lazy, Sunday morning: a street filled with bright shops, merchants sweeping the sidewalks, families heading to church, women shopping in the fruit markets—and no crime. Maybe the bad guys were still in bed.

Farther south, San Fernando Road is jammed with car dealers and auto parts shops, all guarded by high, black iron fences and junk-yard dogs that bark and snarl at passers by.

I was happy the fences were there. I think some of the dogs were, too. One of them growled and frothed menacingly as though he'd tear me to shreds if only he could get through the fence. Then he (or she) ran right past an open gate to growl and froth some more.

Pedro Indacochea's sheep from the high country

It's a different world in Burbank, where tourists and shoppers mingle in trendy stores and restaurants at an open-air mall and on the tree-lined main street that had a homier feel. If you're chilly, there's an indoor mall too. I didn't bother to check the prices in Burbank. The trip was close to the end and so was my bank account.

In downtown LA, men wore jackets and ties; women had high heals and business suits. They were sipping lattes and shopping at Brooks Brothers. It's only 50 miles from San Fernando and 100 miles from the Sierras but what a different world.

Figueroa Street runs south near Watts and Compton where the reputation for crime is worse than San Fernando. Now you're only a few miles from downtown, but still a world apart. Many folks in south LA greeted with me smiles and nods even though I was dressed like Crocodile Dundee. Maybe they weren't smiling, maybe they were laughing.

Then there's the ocean at Long Beach with the Queen Mary, bike paths, oil rigs in the harbor and people greeting me at the end of my journey. It's yet another world—and a very nice one.

Benton Station
Benton

The Benton Paiute tribe literally owns downtown Benton, near the Nevada border. Of course, downtown is little more than a combination store, restaurant and gas stop called Benton Station, which the tribe purchased 20 years ago. It's not a big money-maker, but it is an asset.

"What this does is provide jobs for the people here," said manager Tommy Race, who's been working at the station since the tribe bought it.

Althea Rambeau, one of the restaurant's regular customers, said she came to Benton for a simple life.

"In summer there are a lot of tourists, but mostly it's quiet. There are a lot of good people here," she said.

Kathie Kortering built a house in Benton six years ago after tiring of the bustle in the ski center of Mammoth Lake.

"In Benton kids can ride their bikes on the street, they can have animals and the schools are good," she said.

Kathie and her daughter walked 15 miles with me as I entered California. It made the day pass easily.

The original town of Benton is on Route 120, a few miles east of Benton Station. Today it consists of a bed and breakfast inn built on a hot spring. Feel the floor of your room; it's warmed by the spring. Imagine stepping out of bed onto a toasty floor on a cold morning. If you want to get right to the source, there's a hot spring tub in the back yard. I could have stayed there all day.

Owens Valley
Bishop

When I crossed Montgomery Pass at the Nevada border, I expected California to look like Eden. Unfortunately, it looked like Nevada, which is definitely not Eden. But that changed the next day when I reached seductive, green Owens Valley, nestled between two high mountain ranges. From here on, I would follow the valley south instead of crossing mountains.

When I entered the valley, the Sierra Nevadas had a shawl of puffy clouds wrapped around their shoulders, below their snow-capped peaks. There was a mirror image to the east, where the tall White Mountains frame the other side the narrow valley near the tourist town of Bishop, 270 miles north of L.A. From here you can touch a glacier at noon, explore eerie Mono Lake, and then visit the Devil's Golf Course in Death Valley before dinner.

When California discontinued most of its portion of Route 6 in the 1960s, Bishop became the western end of 6. There's a sign just north of town that says "Provincetown, Mass. 3,205 miles." My feet claim that it's a lot farther.

The smaller towns down the valley were a very friendly. In Lone Pine, the desk clerk at Trails Motel chatted with me for more than a half-hour. In Independence, Michael Patron and his wife, Malika Adjaoud, wouldn't let me go until they treated me to dinner at their restaurant, Still Life.

It was a wonderful dinner, but I was more interested in their story. Michael came here from French wine country and was working as a house painter when he met Malika in Los Angeles. Before they opened the restaurant, they lived in Darwin, a town of about 40 people near Death Valley.

"Darwin is on a dead-end road," Michael said. "People drive down to see what's there. There's nothing to see, so they turn around and go back."

But for Malika, an Algerian, Darwin felt like home.

"The desert was the only place I felt really peaceful. We had no TV, no radio," she said. "The first morning I was there, I woke up and saw snow on the mountain tops. I had the impression of being in North Africa."

Left—Joe and Travis; Above—Malika Adjaoud at Still Life **223**

California Cowboys
Lone Pine, Newhall, Santa Clarita

Maybe they should call California's old Route 6 the movie highway.

The Alabama Hills near Lone Pine attract film crews like a canvass lures an artist. The unusual, almost eerie, rock formations here create ideal locations for science fiction films, but they've been the backdrops for movies and television shows of all types — hundreds of them. You can spot the rocks in episodes of the Rockford Files, Star Trek and Twilight Zone. You can see Russell Crowe in front them in Gladiator. Tourists drive into the hills to see locations that were filmed so often they have names like Movie Flats and Movie Road.

Farther south, the city of Santa Clarita is reviving Newhall, a former movie hub near the Sierra Highway and San Fernando Road. Newhall, with its adobe buildings, is the setting for HBO's Deadwood series, but it was once the home of Monogram Studios and later Gene Autry's Melody Ranch studios.

There were so many westerns shot here that Newhall has a Walk of the Western Stars honoring performers such as Clint Eastwood, Jack Palance and Little House's Melissa Gilbert. Each spring the town hosts a week-long cowboy festival.

Although Santa Clarita was destroyed in a nuclear attack on the TV series "24", it is alive and well and remains the home of Six Flags Magic Mountain amusement park and the California Institute of the Arts (CalArts) not to mention several film studios including Walt Disney and Santa Clarita Studios.

Not bad for a city that wasn't incorporated until 1987. Santa Clarita didn't just spring up overnight, of course. The streets, schools, businesses and homes were here long ago. But the city didn't exist until several communities merged into one.

Fortunately, the new city appreciates its cowboy past.

Alabama Hills **225**

Manzanar

Independence

Manzanar National Historic Site seems out of place among the tourist stops along Owens Valley. Manzanar was the first Japanese internment camp during World War II. It's a place to learn something about our history, our culture and ourselves.

Inside the visitor's center you'll see and hear the story of Japanese-Americans from the turn of the 20th century through the war. You'll learn what it was like to live in one of the camps, where most of the prisoners were under 18.

Mostly, you'll walk out with a sense of the fear that gripped Americans after Pearl Harbor. Back then, the nation's emotions ran far higher than they did after the Sept. 11, 2001 attacks. The exhibits depict a people close to paranoia.

A single shelling of a West Coast site by a Japanese sub was portrayed as the "Battle of Los Angeles" in newspapers. Soldiers fired at balloons, thinking they were Japanese planes. The shells fell over Los Angeles, sending the city into panic. It would be funny if it weren't true.

That atmosphere, along with long-standing prejudice against Asians, had people on the West Coast demanding the removal of the Japanese.

They got their wish, even though it turned out the Japanese never posed a threat.

Outside the visitor's center, you can take a short driving tour of the old camp site.

Manzanar is not your typical tourist attraction—it's better.

Manzanar Internment Camp by Ansel Adams (public domain photo)

Goodbye Ol' Pal
Death Valley

**A**fter 3,500 miles, lots of memories, and a continent of man-to-metal bonding, our little Geo Metro died this week. In Death Valley—just a couple of hundred miles short of our goal. This was the car that picked me up each day at the end of the walk and took me back the next morning.

We put down our modern-day horse in Beatty, Nevada. It was a sad day, but we were grateful to the tiny orange car that people said would never make it to California. Ol' Metro fooled them. We crossed the California line last week and rejoiced, not knowing that Metro was on its last legs, or wheels.

When we reached the official end of Route 6 in Bishop, there were just two more goals—a side trip to Death Valley and the walk down old Route 6 to Long Beach.

As we neared the top of the Argus Range in Death Valley National Park, Metro's brakes gave out. The pedal was down to the floor and barely stopped the car.

We were about to learn how easy it was for the early pioneers to make fatal choices. Sometimes one decision puts you on path where the options just get worse and worse.

We should have turned back, but we went forward, not knowing we were about to head down a very steep eight-mile grade filled with switchbacks. We survived, thanks to first gear.

At the bottom of the Argus Mountains, folks at Panamint Springs told us there were two more ranges between us and the town of Beatty on the eastern side of the park. But the Argus range was the worst of the three, so we continued east hoping we'd find brake fluid at Stovepipe Wells village in the heart of Death Valley.

We found brake fluid. It didn't help.

With dwindling options, we headed east, hoping a mechanic would be able to fix Metro's brakes in Beatty. But there were no repair shops in Beatty. Eventually, we found a repair man at a junkyard. He looked at Metro and said the problem would be fairly easy to solve—if we had the parts. It would take two more days to get the parts from Las Vegas, 120 miles away.

By now we were pretty much locked into an arrival date at Long Beach so there was no time to heal Ol' Metro, and my niece had offered to let us use her camper.

We left our pal sitting there on a jack with its right rear tire bleeding fluid. The mechanic said he'd fix Metro and give it to an elderly woman who needed a car for grocery shopping. That made it easier.

The camper was nearly new. It had air conditioning, a heater that worked, a radio, and lots of other things that Ol' Metro didn't.

But Metro had something no fancy new car will ever have: a shared life. It carried us across a nation, when people said we—humans and car—wouldn't make it. It was a gutsy little vehicle.

Goodbye Ol' Metro. Maybe that little old lady will treat you better than we could.

227

Valley of Death
Death Valley, California

f you've never been to Death Valley, you might picture it as a vast, hot sea of sand, but desert rats like Dave Heffner know there's a lot more to it.

"I've been wandering here 40 years and I still haven't seen it all—and I never will," Dave said.

Death Valley National Park covers three million acres—well beyond the actual valley—and there are spots where few humans have set foot. There are remote canyons, steep snowy mountains, surprising water holes, fiery sunsets, and starry, starry nights. But it's the enormous solitude that makes the area special.

"It gets so quiet, you feel you're going to float right off the face of the earth," Dave said.

It's a place were contrast is common; where the sun turns canyons into kaleidoscopes of color and shadow. There were two feet of snow in the mountains the first day Dave entered the valley. The next day, it was 94 out on the sand dunes.

Other deserts have their own lure, but none beckons the American imagination like Death Valley. We empathize with the pioneers who nearly died here 150 years ago and gave the valley its name.

Then there's the lore of 20-mule teams that hauled borax out of the desert to the town of Mojave. Boraxo paraded mule teams through cities and towns across the nation a century ago to promote soap.

Later, the crack of the mule driver's whip and the creak of the wagon wheels were weekly staples on the "Death Valley Days" radio and television programs.

Dave was among the millions of people who listened to the radio shows.

"I had to imagine what Death Valley looked like. I thought it was flat, with sand dunes," he said with a chuckle.

A lot of people have misconceptions about Death Valley. I pictured a place so vast that people died trying to cross it. The valley, itself, is narrow. You can walk across it in a few hours. But once you're in, there's no easy way out. It's a Venus fly trap.

In 1849, about 300 people left Salt Lake City in search of California gold. One of them had a map that showed a shortcut through Nevada into California.

Well, there are lots of mountains and deserts between Salt Lake and southern California. When the 49ers crossed the Funeral Mountains into the valley they were exhausted and their supplies were nearly gone. Across the valley were even higher mountains that seemed to stretch north and south forever. They could either look for a way to cross the mountains or head down the valley.

The group split up. One party headed south, not knowing that the desert stretched for hundreds of miles into Mexico. They would have died there, but two young men went ahead and brought back provisions just in time.

The other party wandered through the desert searching for a place to cross the mountains. Out of food, they slaughtered their cattle and burned their wagons to cook the meat.

Eventually, they found a pass and, as they crossed the mountains one woman looked back and said: "Goodbye to the valley of death."

The name stuck.

In 1949, Death Valley enthusiasts planned a 100th anniversary celebration of that unfortunate pilgrimage.

Unless you're really, really old you probably don't know a thing about the celebration. But it was the Woodstock of that generation. Organizers expected maybe 15,000 visitors. More than 100,000 people arrived, even though police closed the roads early in the day.

It was so popular that people returned the next year. And folks have been coming back ever since. Every year around Memorial Day hundreds of modern-day 49ers from all over the world gather here to celebrate Death Valley.

I wonder what the woman who named the valley would think of that.

Mosaic Canyon, Death Valley **229**

Boraxo
Death Valley

n the early days of television, a cracking whip and creaking wheels announced the start of Death Valley Days, a long-running show about, well, Death Valley.

The whip and wheels were the sound of twenty-mule teams carrying borax from Death Valley to the railroad junction at Mojave, 160 miles away.

Back in the late 1800s, borax was like a wonder drug. People used it as an elixir to aid digestion, to improve complexion, to remove dandruff, cure diseases and sweeten milk. Even today old folks remember Boraxo, a gritty powdered soap that would just about scour the skin off your hands. It was worse than washing with gravel. Greasy mechanics loved it, kids hated it.

Of course, everybody loved the mule teams. Boraxo paraded them through city streets 100 years ago to market the soap. Later the company used them as their radio and television symbols. Death Valley is, after all, the world's leading source of borax, a white powdery mineral containing boric acid and salt.

The romance of mule teams would have seemed pretty far-fetched to the men who drove the teams over deserts and mountains to reach Mojave. You wouldn't see much romance either, if you were baking in 130-degree temperatures with no shade and little water.

And they certainly wouldn't have thought anyone would travel to Death Valley just for the fun of it. Nevertheless, tens of thousands of folks visit the Death Valley each year and most of them want to hear about those mule teams hauling ten tons of borax.

The mule teams must have been quite a sight rumbling across the desert and over the Panamint Mountains in awkward but sturdy 20-foot long wagons with seven-foot high rear wheels encased in an inch of iron.

The combination of mules and wagons captured the nation's imagination. They were symbols of the desert long after the mule trains were replaced by railroads. They were displayed at the World's Fair in 1904 and at President Woodrow Wilson's inauguration in 1917. More recently they were at the Tournament of Roses Parade in 1999, more than 80 years after they won first place in the Rose Parade—presumably with different mules.

Of course, the 20-mule team was as much marketing as history. To start with, the teams had various numbers of animals and there were often horses on the team. In any case, the teams did the dirty work for only five years before the railroads took over.

At the Furnace Creek Visitors Center, park rangers take visitors on a short walk to point out some of the borax mining highlights and tell a few mining stories, like the one about the young man young man who traveled west to make his fortune. He never struck gold, but he found a good job in the Coffin Mine in Death Valley.

Excited that he was earning money, he wrote to his parents saying: "I'm working at the Coffin Mine in the Funeral Mountains in Death Valley."

There's no record of whether his parents were comforted by the note.

Poor Route 6. It's Lost
Bishop to Long Beach

Poor Route 6, it travels all the way from Cape Cod to California, then gets lost just short of the Pacific Ocean. Sort of like Moses and the Promised Land.

Here's what happened to our favorite road: once upon a time, the highway between Bishop and China Lake was both Route 6 and 395. But in the 1960s, California wanted every road to have just one route number, so the state eliminated Route 6. In fact, bureaucrats got rid of almost all of Route 6 across the state. Instead of Route 6, we now have combination of 395 and 14 from Bishop to Los Angeles, then an assortment of streets from LA to the Pacific Coast Highway and Long Beach.

That change cost Route 6 its title as America's longest road and its status as a coast to coast highway. Poor Route 6.

That was a long time ago, of course, and you won't find many folks who remember old 6. You won't find it on maps, brochures, or highway signs except for a small stretch between the Nevada border and Bishop, which is still Route 6.

Now here's the good news. In 2005 a group of Route 6 enthusiasts convinced the state to designate old Route 6 as a historic highway. Drive through Lancaster and other spots and you'll find historic Route 6 signs along the road.

In fact, Fred Hann, executive director of the California Route 6 Tourist Association, intends to put the signs all along the old 6. "I want people to know it's a historical road. People look for that kind of thing when they're visiting an area," he said.

Hann, the former mayor of Lancaster, was born in Indiana, but he's been in California long enough to remember when Route 6 signs lined the main street.

"I remember when the Route 6 signs came down," he said.

Now, he's seeing them go up again.

Lucky Route 6.

A Taste of Home
Lancaster

**O**n most weekdays, you'll find Barbara Yamamoto preparing dinner for her "family": the

guests at the Inn at Lancaster, on the Sierra Highway.

I've been to scores of hotels across the nation but none has offered a free sit-down dinner five nights a week. The dinners are one of the personal touches Barbara added when she became manager at the Inn 20 years ago. You'll also find cookies, coffee and videos in the reception area, breakfast in the dining room and a security guard watching your car at night.

Barbara says it's just good business. Treat people well and they'll come back.

"We have an 80 percent occupancy rate," she said.

But folks who know Barbara say it's more than business.

"She's like a mom to everybody," said Lenny, the night desk clerk.

Many of the inn's customers are young men and women from the nearby military bases; some of them away from home for the first time. Barbara keeps a close eye on them. They call her "mom."

"I try to make them feel comfortable. They're all my little people," she said.

A few weeks ago the inn got a letter from one of its customers who praised the staff then said "and say thank-you to that sweet lady who cooks the food."

Barbara says it's just business, but I think it's about faith; faith that people are worth caring for and caring about.

Barbara and Sue at the Inn at Lancaster celebrate Thanksgiving with their guests.

Mothballed airliners at Mojave

Mojave

Mojave has just one main street, with stores on the east side and railroad tracks on the west. There are more railroad tracks behind the stores and still more tracks cutting in from the north. Mojave was, and is, a transportation center.

If you walked down the main street 115 years ago, you might see long teams of mules and horses hauling huge wagons of borax from the desert to the train station.

Today, Mojave is the home of the Civilian Aerospace Test Center, which attracts air buffs, test pilots and engineers from around the world.

"It's the only nonmilitary space pilot testing center in the world that I know of," said Bill Deaver, president of the town council and editor of the weekly newspaper.

The airfield was a flight testing and training site during World War II and the Korean War. But when military projects faded, the town recruited private companies, some of them contractors at nearby Edwards Air Force Base, who wanted to do their own testing.

Now little Mojave is a Mecca for all sorts of aircraft.

"If you like planes, this is heaven," Bill said. "You can look up in the sky and see just about anything."

Military cargo planes land and go; a Stealth bomber occasionally buzzes the airport. Spaceship One, the first private manned mission to space, was developed and launched here. Voyager, the first plane to fly around the world without refueling, was built here.

You can sit in the Voyager Restaurant next to the tarmac and watch test planes taking off and landing. You can hear the control tower chatter from speakers at your table. There's a good chance you'll be sitting near pilots from countries that don't have their own programs to train test pilots.

On the airfield, you might see privately owned Russian MIGs, or vintage World War I planes. Last week, two British Tiger Moth WWII training planes flew into the airfield. Before that, a Russian AN124, one

of the world's largest cargo planes, stopped by.

Now here's the strangest sight at the airfield—dozens of jumbo jets seemingly abandoned with their logos covered and their windshields shuttered. This is where the airlines store their unneeded planes. It left me with an eerie feeling, like walking by a giant graveyard. "You can tell the health of the airline industry by how many planes we have here," Bill said.

Hopefully, these jumbos aren't dead, just resting.

About 25 miles down the road, you might get a closer look at Stealth bombers and fighters in Lancaster, where the Stealths were built and where they return for maintenance.

Just off the Sierra Highway (which was once Route 6) people gather almost daily in a vacant lot in Lancaster to watch the military planes come and go at Plant 42 which handles Air Force special projects. The Space Shuttle was built here.

Across the street, B. J. McWorten turned plane watching into an art form in the late 1980s.

"He'd spend his days out there and when there was something special going on he'd tell his friends. There'd be 150 people out there watching," said Bill Warford, a columnist for the Antelope Valley News in nearby Palmdale.

Even today, when you see large crowds in the lot you know something's in the works at Plant 42. B.J. died a few years ago, but plane spotters still gather in the vacant lot—right next to the flag planted there in B. J's memory.

Now you're wondering what makes this area so attractive to fliers, airlines and the Air Force. It's the desert. The dry air helps preserve those mothballed jetliners and the predictably clear skies mean few weather delays for training and test flights.

Clean, Green—and very big
Los Angeles

Here's a riddle: What's clean, green and very, very big. The answer is Los Angeles, of course.

I was in LA only a few days, but even a few weeks might not be enough to see all of this sprawling city. You could spend most of that time touring film sites like the Hollywood Walk of Fame, Grauman's Chinese Theater, the studios and the Hollywood sign. But there's a lot more to LA: the farmers market, Griffiths Park, the Watts Towers, Venice, Rodeo Drive and the La Brea tar pits, where so many creatures were mummified after being trapped in the sticky tar.

You get the idea, LA is very big.

If you visit Chinatown stop and look at the streets. They're clean. You can thank Rudy Gonzalez and friends for that.

Every morning Rudy drives a street cleaner through Chinatown, then he leads a team of a half-dozen teen-agers through the roads in search of trash. He's a program coordinator for the Los Angeles Conservation Corps' Clean and Green Program.

The teens, working for minimum wage, sweep the streets, bag trash and toss the bags into the back of Rudy's pick-up truck.

"We get about 90 bags a day, but it's a lot more on weekends when the tourists are in town," Rudy said. "It would help if people put their trash in the containers."

He's just 22, but Rudy's been working in the program for eight years, so he has an idea of why these kids sign up. It's not just for the money.

"These are good kids. I give them a lot of credit. They'd rather come to work than stay home and do nothing," he said. Most of the teens volunteer for the program though their school.

The kids come from tough sections of the city. Some are happy to be in another part of town, but Robert Ortega, of East L.A., would rather work closer to home and improve his own neighborhood.

"There should be more programs like this," said one of the students. They all agreed.

The teens were brimming with smiles when I met them on York Street. But it's not all fun and games.

"You get a lot garbage on you," Robert said.

Walk maybe five miles from Chinatown on Figueroa Street and you'll be in South Los Angeles. That's where I heard the foot-tapping, hand-clapping rhythm of drums beckoning from the parking lot at The House of Uhuru near 80th Street.

There were two dozen people practicing their steps for the upcoming Martin Luther King Parade. It's a march that could help change their lives.

Uhuru is a private organization that helps people overcome drug and alcohol problems.

About two dozen of the center's clients march in the parade each year. For them this is therapy.

"It motivates them to participate in community events," said Alton Hammond, a social worker at the center. Hammond said many clients think of themselves as outcasts.

"Here they get out of their image. They participate in a community event. Their community spirit is awakened," he said.

It sounds like happy-talk, but Hammond said he's seen it happen and he sees people every year whose eyes light up when they march in the parade.

That sparkle in their eyes is called hope.

One man built the Watts Towers (left) in Los Angeles using scrap metal and broken pottery. Above—Rudy Gonzalez and teens keep LA clean.

Queen of the Sea
Long Beach

I followed Figueroa Street past Watts and down to the Pacific Coast Highway.

Silly me, I thought the coast highway was a scenic road. Not this section, unless you consider refineries, motels, discount stores and fast food spots scenic.

Just a few blocks from the PCH, downtown Long Beach was closer to what I had in mind. My wife joined me in Long Beach We rented bikes and rode along the shoreline bike path. We visited the aquarium and we browsed the shops in Shoreline Village. We watched the ships coming and going.

But nothing matched the Queen Mary. Ok, that's an exaggeration; watching the sun set over the Pacific was pretty nice, too.

The Queen Mary was once one of the biggest, fastest and most famous ocean liners in the world. That was when crossing the Atlantic took weeks, and ordinary folks would never see the Queen Mary, much less sail on it.

So it was a little humbling for me to spend a couple of nights on this icon of the good life. It's one of the many things that I've been able to do that were only dreams for working class people a generation or two before me. Unfortunately, these special things are rarely as elegant by the time I get to them. It's like finding fancy, but faded, clothes at the thrift shop. Nonetheless, I was thrilled to be on this legendary ship.

The Queen no longer sails the oceans. She's permanently docked at Long Beach as a combination hotel, tourist attraction and maritime museum. The ship was destined for the scrap heap when Long Beach bought it.

Many of the luxuries, such as the pool and stately dining rooms have been replaced by more practical shops and eateries. But still, you feel special walking along the wide decks and through narrow corridors below deck —or just lounging in an ocean-side chair and reading a book as the world slowly passes by.

You can tour the ship as a hotel guest or day visitor. You can imagine you're on a two-week crossing in the 1930s or that you're a soldier making the journey during World War II when the QM was a troop carrier. They say the big ship was so fast that German U-boats couldn't track her.

You can even try to imagine what it was like when a giant wave almost capsized the Queen Mary. That scary incident was inspiration for the Poseidon Adventure.

Or you can pretend that you're an actor in one of the many movies and television shows shot aboard the ship, including Titanic.

Hmm. U-boats. Titanic. Poseidon. I think I'll move closer to shore.

Joe and Travis at the Queen Mary